W9-DDN-773

REMBRANDT HARMENSZ VAN RIJN

REMBRANDT. SELF-PORTRAIT. Etching. 1639   The Hermitage, Leningrad

Rembrandt Harmensz van Rijn

PAINTINGS FROM SOVIET MUSEUMS

HARRY N. ABRAMS, INC., PUBLISHERS, NEW YORK
AURORA ART PUBLISHERS, LENINGRAD

Edited by VLADIMIR LOEWINSON-LESSING

Introductory articles by
VLADIMIR LOEWINSON-LESSING and
XENIA YEGOROVA

Notes on the plates by
YURY KUZNETSOV (2, 3, 5—7, 9—17)
IRENE LINNIK (4, 19, 21, 22, 24, 25, 27—30)
XENIA YEGOROVA (1, 8, 18, 20, 23, 26)

Translated from the Russian by
VLADIMIR POZNER

Designed by ALEXANDER DURANDIN

4th edition, revised

The technical analysis of Rembrandt's paintings was
conducted in the Pushkin Museum of Fine Arts by
the staff of the Central Research Laboratory for
Preservation and Restoration: M. Vikturina, A. Dub
and E. Stepanov; in the Hermitage Museum by
L. Siverskov, Head of the X-ray laboratory.

International Standard Book Number: 0-8109-1564-2

© 1981 by Aurora Art Publishers, Leningrad

Printed and bound in the USSR

ON THE HISTORY OF THE COLLECTION
OF REMBRANDT'S PAINTINGS IN SOVIET MUSEUMS

The collection of Rembrandt's paintings in Soviet museums is one of the most outstanding in the world. It is concentrated in the Hermitage Museum, Leningrad; six more paintings are to be found in the Pushkin Museum of Fine Arts, Moscow. The Russian collection has long enjoyed world fame, being considered, in the nineteenth and early twentieth centuries, the world's finest both in quantity and quality.

Since then, certain changes have taken place. The leading American museums have greatly increased their collections. With the advance of knowledge, many works formerly attributed to Rembrandt have been found to belong to his pupils. Nevertheless, the Soviet collection remains one of the finest. It could not be otherwise with a collection of such exceptional quality, the vast majority of the paintings of which are so well preserved and so varied, a collection that contains such masterpieces as *Danaë* and *The Return of the Prodigal Son*.

The first Rembrandt painting appeared in Russia during the rule of Peter the Great, who laid the foundations of Western European art collections in Russia. He began this project during his first trip abroad in 1697, when his interest was aroused by the works of Dutch marine painters. Sent to Holland in 1715, Yury Kologrivov acquired 43 paintings at The Hague for the decoration of the Tsar's summer palace of Monplaisir, then under construction in Peterhof. This was followed by the purchase of 117 paintings in Brussels and Antwerp. Similar instructions were given to B. Kurakin, the Russian ambassador to The Hague, and to Osip Solovyov, the Russian Trade Commissar in Amsterdam. On June 30, 1716, Solovyov sent to St Petersburg 121 paintings "bought at public and private sales". In the list accompanying the letter, we find mentioned Rembrandt's *David's Farewell to Jonathan*, acquired, as was recently established, at the auction of Jan van Beuningen's collection in Amsterdam for the price of 80 guldens. This was a time when the voices of Rembrandt's sworn enemies in art rang loud, when they lifted their heads after his death and labelled him "the greatest heretic in art". Due to the efforts of those who defended the academic aesthetic principles, Rembrandt's paintings, no longer popular, were rarely put up for sale and sold at very low prices, as in the above-described case.

The sixties of the eighteenth century opened a new page in the history of Russian art collections. It was then that the Winter Palace picture gallery was born; it grew with such speed that in the span of two decades it gained a pre-eminent place among Europe's art collections.

The first collection of paintings was acquired for the Hermitage in 1764. Johann Ernst Gotzkowsky, a Berlin merchant, offered his paintings in payment of a debt to the Russian treasury. The Gotzkowsky collection, brought to St Petersburg in the summer of 1764, numbered 225 paintings, mainly of the Dutch and Flemish schools. Although the general level of that collection was not very high, it did include some works of great artistic merit. Among these were two canvases by Rembrandt: *The Incredulity of St Thomas* and *Ahasuerus, Haman and Esther* (both in the Pushkin Museum of Fine Arts, Moscow).

5

The most active role in enriching the new gallery's collection was to be played by Prince Dmitry Golitsyn, sent to Paris in 1765 as *chargé d'affaires*, and, in 1768, to The Hague as ambassador. Golitsyn was one of Russia's most cultured men of the second half of the eighteenth century, a personal friend of Denis Diderot and Etienne-Maurice Falconet, honorary member of the St Petersburg Academy of Fine Arts. His first Paris purchases date to 1766—67, when the collections of the painter Aved and the outstanding art collector Jean de Julienne were put up for auction. Among other works acquired was Rembrandt's *Portrait of an Old Woman with Spectacles*. During that same period, Golitsyn managed to buy Rembrandt's celebrated masterpiece, *The Return of the Prodigal Son*. This painting was part of the collection of the Archbishop of Cologne, Elector Clemens Augustus; it was put on sale in Bonn after his death in 1764 and bought by two French dealers, Boileau and Julienne, who took the collection to Paris and auctioned it off in the same year. *The Prodigal Son*, however, remained unsold, and was purchased after the auction by a certain Monsieur d'Amezune for 5,400 livres, together with a painting by Luca Giordano, priced at 600 livres. Golitsyn bought Rembrandt's canvas for a similar or probably a slightly higher price and sent it to St Petersburg. There, the outstanding qualities of this masterpiece did not go unnoticed. In August, 1772, Falconet wrote to Catherine II: "I have received letters from France mentioning a wonderful Rembrandt painting that constitutes a pair to *The Prodigal Son*. If this is really so, then it is worthy of gracing Your Majesty's gallery. If Your Majesty wishes, I will write to one of our finest artists, asking him to look into this matter and see if this canvas really answers the description; naturally, I take care to give this instruction to no one else... The subject of the painting is: *Mordecai at the Feet of Esther and Ahasuerus*, the price, 3,600 livres." "If the painting you speak of," answered Catherine a few days later, "is indeed a pair to my *Prodigal Son*, then I am ready to purchase; the price of 3,600 livres seems to me very moderate..." The painting, however, was not bought. The Secretary of the Paris Academy, Cochin, wrote that the canvas had been in Paris "for 15 years without finding a buyer. To attribute it to the great master would be an insult to his memory." Later the picture was attributed to Rembrandt's school. It is now in the Bucharest Museum of Fine Arts.

An event of major importance in the history of the Hermitage picture gallery was the acquisition, in 1769, of the collection of Count Heinrich Brühl, all-powerful minister of August III of Saxony. Brühl admitted openly that he was no connoisseur of art, and depended entirely on the taste and decisions of his secretary, Heinrich von Heinecken, a well-known art critic who, in 1746, became head of the Print Room and *de facto* ran the Dresden Picture Gallery. Having published in 1754 a selection of engravings after his finest items, Brühl sent them to important persons abroad, among them to M. I. Vorontsov and I. I. Shuvalov in Russia. After Brühl's death in 1764, his belongings were sequestrated; consequently the talks begun between the count's heirs and A. M. Beloselsky-Belozersky, the Russian ambassador to the Saxonian court, a connoisseur of art and art collector, had to be broken off until 1769. After that, the talks were brought to a satisfactory conclusion: four Rembrandt paintings from the Brühl collection went to Russia. Two of them, *Portrait of a Scholar* and *Portrait of an Old Man in Red*, counted among the artist's finest works, are in the Hermitage, while *Portrait of Adriaen van Rijn* and *Portrait of an Old Woman* belong, since 1929, to the Pushkin Museum collection.

In 1769, the John Blackwood collection, consisting of 43 paintings, was bought in London through the banker Friedrichs. The list of its items has not yet been discovered, and the provenance of only one painting from this collection could be established. This is the picture known at present as *David and Uriah* (Hermitage). The name of its former owner was indicated on a mezzotint

6

done by R. Houston after this work of Rembrandt, in those times called *The Downfall of Haman*. One of the relatively few cases when the exact date and circumstances of a painting's acquisition remain obscure is that of *Flora*, put on sale in 1770 at the auction of Harmen Arents' collection in Amsterdam and included in the Hermitage catalogue of 1774. In all probability, it was bought by D. A. Golitsyn. While living in Holland, Golitsyn retained many contacts in Paris. François Tronchin of Geneva, whose collection was acquired by Catherine II in 1770 and who had close ties with Golitsyn, informed him and Diderot that the heiresses of Baron de Thiers, the last owner of the famous Crozat gallery who had made several valuable additions to his uncle's collection, were willing to sell the pictures. Tronchin managed to convince them not to auction the collection but to sell it *in toto* to the Russian Empress. The talks were concluded in 1772, and the collection was sent to St Petersburg.

Pierre Crozat was a very rich financier who made his fortune in his home city of Toulouse, from whence he and his brother Antoine moved to Paris in 1704. In Paris, Pierre Crozat soon dropped his commercial activity so as to give all his time to his one passion: collectioning. His gallery included paintings of different schools, and boasted masterpieces of the greatest painters. A refined connoisseur, he relied mainly on his own taste, turning for advice only to his friend Pierre Mariette, a specialist in the field of drawing. According to the Tronchin inventory, the gallery had twelve Rembrandt paintings, eight of which are now the property of the Hermitage: today, four of these are attributed to the Rembrandt school. The most important of all is Rembrandt's masterpiece, *Danaë*. Then come his *Holy Family with Angels*, *The Labourers in the Vineyard* and, finally, his small and earliest painting, *The Old Warrior*. Pierre Crozat cannot be blamed for attributing to the great Dutch master several works by his pupil, Ferdinand Bol: the critical analysis of Rembrandt's legacy began only in the last quarter of the nineteenth century.

Another very important acquisition was that of the Robert Walpole collection in Houghton Hall, England, extremely rich in seventeenth century paintings. It included two canvases by Rembrandt: *Abraham's Sacrifice* (Hermitage) and *Portrait of an Old Woman* (Pushkin Museum).

The Russian Rembrandt collection was enriched in 1781 by the acquisition of the Paris collection of Count de Baudouin, Brigadier of the Royal Forces. This was done through Frédéric-Melchior, Baron de Grimm, who replaced Diderot as Catherine's correspondent and agent. Baudouin, who amassed his collection over a forty-year period, told Grimm in a letter dated March 14, 1780, that he had finished working on its catalogue. He wrote: "The idea of parting with my collection came to my mind only after speaking to you. If Her Majesty refuses your offer to buy my collection, please keep the entire affair secret. I will prepare 20 prints of the finest of my paintings for publication." On April 7 of the following year, reaffirming his readiness to sell his collection, Baudouin wrote that Russian art lovers, to whom he had shown his picture gallery, could tell the Empress of its qualities. The collection was bought in 1781 and sent to St Petersburg together with the manuscript catalogue. It had many fine Rembrandt paintings, including such Hermitage canvases as *Portrait of an Old Man*, *Portrait of an Old Woman*, *Young Woman with Earrings*, *Portrait of the Poet Jeremias de Decker*, and *Jacob's Sons Show Their Father Joseph's Bloody Coat*, attributed to Rembrandt's school.

Two more Rembrandt paintings entered the Hermitage in the eighteenth century: *Portrait of Baertjen Martens Doomer*, of obscure origin, and *Christ and the Woman of Samaria* from the collection of Prince G. A. Potemkin-Tavrichesky, bought in 1792. Potemkin's large gallery, built up by purchases from dealers in St Petersburg and partly from the Duchess of Kingston, was of very unequal quality. This gallery contained, as was recently established, Rembrandt's *Christ and*

7

the Woman of Samaria, wrongly believed to come from the Blackwood collection. The engraving which mentions Blackwood as the owner, was made from another painting on the same subject, now in Berlin.

In 1814, Alexander I acquired from the Empress Josephine her gallery of Malmaison. It included several paintings of the famous Cassel Gallery, among them *The Descent from the Cross* by Rembrandt. Before coming to Cassel, these paintings were the property of Mrs. Roever of Delft and were bought with the rest of her collection by Ludwig VII, Landgrave of Hesse-Cassel. The Cassel Gallery was taken by Napoleon in 1806 and presented to Josephine. The successor of Ludwig VII, an ally of Alexander in the Napoleonic wars, in 1815 demanded that the Cassel paintings be returned. Alexander vigorously refuted these claims, for he had paid for the paintings and was very attentive to Josephine and her daughter Hortense. In 1829, Hortense, officially called Duchess of Saint-Leu after her divorce with Louis Bonaparte, sold to the Russian Emperor thirty paintings inherited by her from her mother. Among them was Rembrandt's *Portrait of a Young Man with a Lace Collar*. In 1852, at the sale of the collection of Count of Morgny (second son of Hortense) in Paris, Rembrandt's *Portrait of an Old Man* was bought by F. A. Bruni, at that time head of the Hermitage picture gallery.

After the October Revolution of 1917, the State Museum Reserve added to the Hermitage collection Rembrandt's *Adoration of the Magi*, which had belonged to I. I. Paskevich (née Countess Vorontsova-Dashkova). The Vorontsov-Dashkov family possessed a famous art gallery, founded in the first half of the nineteenth century.

In 1915, at the exhibition of paintings by old Western European masters from private collections held in the Rumiantsev Museum, Moscow, there was one painting from the collection of P. C. Giraud, attributed to Rembrandt's school: *Christ Driving the Money-changers from the Temple*. In 1924 it became the property of the Pushkin Museum and later was recognized as a genuine work of Rembrandt.

Two paintings are not included in this edition: *Judith at Her Toilet* and *Study of a Man's Head*. The first, attributed to Rembrandt in the Hermitage catalogue of Western European painting (1958), has now been proved to belong to his school. The second, previously attributed to Rembrandt with a question mark, is now known to be by Carel Fabritius.

The beginning of a critical analysis of Rembrandt's pictorial heritage finds its source in the seventies of the last century. It is associated with the name of Wilhelm Bode, the outstanding German art historian, and with the names of two eminent Dutch specialists, Abraham Bredius and C. Hofstede de Groot. The activities of these three prominent "Rembrandtologists" encompass a sixty-year period. Bode, who had carefully studied the Hermitage collection, as well as the most important private collections of St Petersburg, accorded the former no small role in his *Studien zur Geschichte der holländischen Malerei* (Braunschweig, 1883). Bredius and Hofstede de Groot were also well acquainted with the Hermitage's Dutch paintings; they gave much time to the gathering and publication of letters and documents related to Rembrandt's life and work. Hofstede de Groot's *Urkunden über Rembrandt* (The Hague, 1906) to this day retains its significance.

The publication of reproductions, with detailed notes, of all of Rembrandt's canvases was first accomplished by Bode, with the participation of Hofstede de Groot, in 1897—1905: *The Complete Works of Rembrandt* in 8 volumes were published in Paris on a donation of C. Sedelmeyer, one of the most important art dealers of the time. In the sixth volume of his *Beschreibendes und kritisches Verzeichnis der Werke der hervorragendsten holländischen Maler des XVII. Jahrhunderts* (1915), de Groot provided every painting with a complete list of references made to it in documents, auction catalogues, etc., thus bringing to light each canvas's origin and subsequent history; his inventory includes all presently known paintings and their whereabouts, as well as data on paintings that cannot today be linked to any known work.

A volume of reproductions was published by the German art historian and critic Wilhelm Valentiner in 1909. This album included 643 paintings. In 1921 and 1923 Valentiner, who made his home in the United States, published an additional volume that contained 100 more recently discovered paintings. In 1935, A. Bredius published what he considered to be the ultimate list of authentic Rembrandt paintings: altogether 620 works (*Rembrandt. Gemälde*, Phaidon-Verlag, Wien). H. Gerson, who began his career working with Bredius on the above-mentioned publication and who is now a professor at Groningen University and one of the leading authorities on Rembrandt and his school, published a revised edition of Bredius's work (*Rembrandt. The Complete Edition of the Paintings*, London), in which the number of the authentic works is put at 630. At the same time, in notes to this publication Gerson stated his doubts concerning the authenticity of several canvases, and narrowed the number of paintings he believed to be genuine to 450. K. Bauch, who visited the Soviet Union as a young scholar, and who is now a university professor at Freiburg im Breisgau, published in 1966 a large volume (*Rembrandt. Gemälde*, Berlin) which includes both Rembrandt's universally acknowledged works and those that are questioned. Gerson and Bauch had the possibility to carefully study the Soviet collection of Rembrandt paintings (incidentally, it was Gerson who identified *Christ Driving the Money-changers from the Temple* as a Rembrandt work). The Hermitage collection was also examined by Jakob Rosenberg, an authority on Rembrandt's art. Of pre-revolutionary Russian specialists in that field, the most important contribution was made by A. I. Somov, long-time head of the Hermitage picture gallery. In 1902 he published his *Catalogue of Dutch and Flemish Paintings*.

During the Soviet period, the exhibitions of 1939, 1956 and 1969, which included the works of Rembrandt, as well as those of his teachers and pupils, played an important role in the further study of the Dutch master's art.

This edition, besides giving a complete publication of Rembrandt's paintings in the Soviet Union, was meant to sum up, at least partially, the study of these works. Nowadays the most up-to-date methods of research are widely applied in the field of Rembrandt studies: documentary evidence and the data furnished by stylistic analysis are examined in the light of modern restoration techniques which include the use of X-ray, infra-red and ultraviolet photography. Such methods permit to form a more adequate idea of the great master's working process and of the subjects of his pictures; they help to establish the identity of his models and allow for more precise datings. Results of primary importance have been furnished by Rembrandt studies at the Hermitage. The history of the famous *Danaë*, one of the artist's masterpieces, has been fully reconstructed; the long-forgotten *Adoration of the Magi* has found its proper place in Rembrandt's œuvre; new light has been thrown on such well-known works as *Parable of the Labourers in the Vineyard* and *David's Farewell to Jonathan*.

The latest and most important works by Soviet art specialists are referred to in the Catalogue of this edition. The authors hope that these data will be of interest to both professionals and amateurs of art.

V. Loewinson-Lessing

REMBRANDT'S PAINTINGS
IN SOVIET MUSEUMS

The majority of Rembrandt's paintings in the Soviet Union have one common source — the Hermitage collection, founded toward the end of the eighteenth century. Thus it may be stated that Rembrandt has been "present" in Russian culture for two centuries.

The Hermitage Museum was opened to the public in 1852, but many people, besides the official guests of the Imperial palace, had the opportunity to see the Hermitage collections prior to that date. Entrance permission was easily granted to painters and art lovers. The St Petersburg Academy of Fine Arts included the copying of old masters in its curriculum. Finally, the Hermitage pictures became known to the public through numerous prints.

The second half of the eighteenth century, when the Hermitage collection was in the process of formation, saw a surge of interest in Rembrandt's legacy in Europe. During the age of Romanticism the name of Rembrandt became extremely popular in European intellectual circles, and, interesting to note, this vogue was more apparent in literature than in painting. This was especially characteristic of the situation in Russia, where the painter's name often appeared in works of literature. Alexander Pushkin, for instance, in his poem *The Cottage in Kolomna*, introduced an old widow to the reader with the comment:

> Such faces I have seen a hundred times
> In Rembrandt paintings.

In all probability, the poet considered Rembrandt's paintings as an embodiment of true life touched with prosaic simplicity, while the sublime in "pure beauty" to him was symbolized in Raphael's *Madonna*. Many contemporaries of the poet held a similar view.

However, during that same period a completely different interpretation of Rembrandt finds growing popularity. Its mood is particularly well expressed in Mikhail Lermontov's poem *On a Rembrandt Painting*, written between 1830 and 1831:

> . . . .
> This face, perhaps, is not perfection,
> And for your model you took life!
> Perhaps it was your own reflection
> In years of suffering and strife?
> . . . .
> But no cold eyes will pierce the curtain,
> Nor your great secret dare approach,
> And your strange work will stand, 'tis certain,
> To soulless hearts a grim reproach.

Lermontov probably had in mind the portrait of the painter's son Titus van Rijn as a monk, then part of the Stroganov collection in St Petersburg* (now the property of the Amsterdam

10

---

* According to V. Loewinson-Lessing.

Rijksmuseum). This "strange work" must have fascinated the poet because of the qualities of the model. For Lermontov he is a romantic hero to be identified with the painter himself. The painting is not only an embodiment of art's "great secret", but also of the model's "secret fate"; Lermontov's conjectures bear the stamp of an openly romantic stereotype. Rembrandt's "sombre genius" reflects the poet's own concept of passion, of suffering, of truly unfettered and truly individual creativity, incomprehensible to the "soulless" crowd of mundane art consumers.

The interest in Rembrandt, awakened by the romanticists, was not to be short-lived. When Alexander Herzen, one of Russia's finest minds of the nineteenth century, said of Shakespeare and Rembrandt that he found in their works "a world reflecting life in all its verity and depth, in all its winding passages and byways of light and darkness", he only gave wording to a commonly acknowledged idea. The development of the Russian realistic school of painting in the second half of the nineteenth century, and the corresponding fundamental changes it brought about in art, served to furnish a new understanding and evaluation of the old master. If earlier he was regarded as a "heretic" who chose to swerve from the rules of classical art and follow the arbitrary impulses of his personal creative temperament, the more perspicacious minds of the new democratic culture were quick to discover a deep logic in his artistic idiom. The Russian painter Ivan Kramskoi (1837—1887) considered the Dutch master's work a pinnacle of painting, no less important than that reached in antiquity in the realm of sculpture. Nor was it through abstract speculation that Kramskoi came to this conclusion. Both he and his contemporaries renounced idealized academic drawing and turned to a much freer manner. Theirs was an attempt to convey nature's intrinsic spiritual expressiveness and picturesque beauty, and they saw an analogy to their own search in the Dutch master's heritage. Kramskoi and other artists of his generation viewed with envy the pictures by Rembrandt and Velázquez and dreamed of showing the spiritual essence of their own times through art as strikingly and fully as the great masters of the seventeenth century had done. Yet the Russian painters realized that imitation would not solve the problem, that the world of old art differed vastly from that in which they lived and worked. Here the historical approach, characteristic of nineteenth century thought, fused with conclusions drawn from personal experience.

The gradual change in the interpretation of Rembrandt's art over the nineteenth century not only forms an interesting page in the history of European culture in general and Russian culture in particular; it is also important nowadays. The spiritual heritage of that period possessed an astonishing degree of viability: even today it may set standards where our reactions and evaluations of cultural phenomena are concerned. This is especially true of Rembrandt's art: the basic concepts that crystallized at that time continue to exist today. Certain features of his art seem to have been established once and for all; these are its amazing originality and its incomparable spiritual force, so typical of his mature period. It was also in the nineteenth century that the complex relationship of attraction and alienation between the artist and society began to be understood. Serious study of Rembrandt's art was in its infancy in the nineteenth century. Since then a wealth of data have come to light concerning both the man and his work, his environment and his age. Scholars, time and again, seek to comprehend the very essence of his art and to define its historical role and place in the spiritual heritage of later generations.

Besides absorbing contemporary features, our consciousness preserves the psychological experience amassed by generations long gone. Such is the vital condition of the continuity of culture. If this were not so, all art of the past would be dead to us. However, we are not direct spiritual heirs of Rembrandt: he is separated from us by three full centuries during which the traditional interpretation of his art was evolved. This fact is both an advantage and a disadvantage: it is difficult to look on famous works of art in a way so unbiased as to ignore what we have heard and read thousands of times. Our capacity to enjoy painting is also the result of cultural tradition, in which the legacy of the nineteenth century overshadows all others. A period of fantastic literary development, the nineteenth century introduced what was to become a habit: a narrative interpretation of the visual arts.

There are paintings, and the nineteenth century is no exception, that are virtually devoid of any narrative context. Rembrandt's paintings, on the contrary, as a rule present no obstacle to literary interpretation, yet this is true only to a certain extent. The faces and gestures of his characters speak of many things, they lift the curtain on the model's "life story". However, an attempt to render one's visual impression in words shows the result to be at best only partial. A Rembrandt painting is a highly complicated artistic organism that lives following its own laws; it is an artistic organism that embodies the titanic world of the painter's emotions and thoughts. It appeals to all our feelings, to our imagination and personal experience. Each painting is a unique work of art, but at the same time it is a link in the long chain of the master's creations: at any point of this chain we may find other paintings directly or indirectly tied to the one in question. This article represents an attempt to define the place of Rembrandt's paintings from Soviet museums in the evolution of his art. Since our immediate concern is the Soviet collection of Rembrandts, we have no choice but to refrain from commenting on other aspects of the painter's artistic biography, on his relations with the Dutch art of the period, etc.

The legacy of Rembrandt the painter consists mainly of portraits and canvases on biblical and mythological subjects; such paintings were called "histories" in the seventeenth century. Portraits constitute the majority, but to the painter himself his "histories" were far more important. If we keep in mind the general cultural atmosphere of the age, Rembrandt's predilection for biblical subjects does not call for justification. Nevertheless it needs certain clarification in the framework of Dutch art. Why did Rembrandt, seeing the interest which his countrymen manifested towards genre art, usually ignore it in his paintings, turning to it only in drawings and etchings?

The seventeenth century art tended simultaneously towards a concrete description of reality and to vast generalizations. Notwithstanding the brilliant flowering of artistic genres that reflected the various aspects of reality (landscapes, portraits, etc.), the synthetic genre of "histories" was held in special esteem by the art lovers of that period. "Histories" served as a vehicle for solving important moral, psychological, and social problems. The genre art of the seventeenth century does not, as a rule, venture upon the examination of such problems. Painters would turn for this purpose to contemporary life only in the nineteenth century. Herein lies the reason for Rembrandt's preoccupation with "histories", while genre subjects figure in his minor works, viz. engravings and etchings.

The second most important sphere of his work is the portrait. Close and multiple ties exist between this and his "histories".

Such is the genre structure of Rembrandt's legacy, such is the composition of the Rembrandt collection in Soviet museums.

Rembrandt's emergence as an independent painter is traditionally related to 1625. His earliest works differ strikingly from everything he was to create later. For many years theirs was a fate of oblivion. The last fifty years of our century, however, saw them attract the growing attention of scholars: virgin territory promised interesting discoveries. As a result, several exceptionally original paintings were definitely proved to belong to Rembrandt. Among these, one of the most important is his *Christ Driving the Money-changers from the Temple* (1626, Pushkin Museum). The motley and rather bright colouring was passed on to young Rembrandt by his teacher, Pieter Lastman. The half-length figures of merchants and money-changers pile one on top of the other; they scream as they try to escape or fend off the flailing scourge while saving their money and wares. The anatomy is faulty, the perspective rather doubtful, and yet even in this strange work which boasts neither unity nor harmony, one discerns the fitful internal fire inherent in Rembrandt's work. The painter's intense feelings are even more apparent here than in his later creations, where a great aesthetic culture helps him control his temperament. Human emotions, or "passions", occupied an important place in the spiritual life of the seventeenth century. Men of the world discussed them in salons, philosophers wrote theses on the subject, painters made them the main theme of their art. Thus, when Rembrandt depicted the anger of Christ and the fear and surprise of the merchants, he was tackling a problem of universal interest, but its solution bears the imprint of the artist's individuality. Compared to the abstract and watered-down passions of a theatrical nature that strike the eye in the works of Lastman and many of his contemporaries, the emotions portrayed by the twenty-year-old Rembrandt are stunningly natural and forceful. The young painter looks to life for his inspiration, refuting conventional standards. In the following years, the problem of depicting emotions becomes dominant in Rembrandt's creative endeavours. His concept of man's inner world, as well as of the aesthetic possibilities of painting, grows at an astonishing pace. Before long, works of an exceptionally high professional standard appear; in them one discerns traits that are to become characteristic of Rembrandt's further development as a painter. He shows rising interest in man's intense spiritual life and demonstrates an understanding of the emotional expressiveness of the space-light medium.

Studying the diversity of man's facial expressions, the painter produces several half-length pictures of himself and of two or three relatives or intimates. Working on etchings, he creates a whole series of small "self-portraits grimacing"; the etchings show Rembrandt in an exaggerated state of fear, surprise, jeering laughter, etc. This ironic exaggeration makes one suppose that the generally accepted set of passions seemed primitive to him. In painting, however, his *tronies* (heads), as they came to be known in Dutch auction catalogues, usually convey not a passion but a more stable and meaningful mood, reflecting to a greater or smaller degree the model's nature. Toward the end of the Leyden period the "heads" take on an aspect of real portraits.

One of these is his *Old Warrior* (*ca.* 1630, Hermitage). During the Leyden years this man was one of Rembrandt's constant sitters. We recognize him in the old man dressed in dark, fur-trimmed clothes in *Christ Driving the Money-changers from the Temple*. As a rule, the painter chose this man for depicting nervous, changing moods so helpful to the study of fleeting emotions. However, in the Hermitage canvas the sitter's appearance acquires a somewhat different quality. Rembrandt's artistic manner is already highly refined. The translucent chiaroscuro and hidden movement of the tiny brush-strokes that flow around the figure animate the ugly and original face. The artist is fascinated by textural confrontation in the black gamut: the black silk of the clothing next to the cold surface of the burnished steel, the deep tone of the velvet beret and the dancing pinpoints of light on the ostrich feathers.

The dress does not correspond to the fashion of the times. It is, rather, a Rembrandt invention, composed as it is of details that offer striking textural contrasts. Visual and pictorial expressiveness, however, was not the painter's sole purpose: in his eyes these contrasts helped to elevate the subject from the commonplace to a loftier plane. The steel breastplate was an accessory of a warrior's portrait, while the feathered beret was an integral part of the so-called "Burgundy"

13

dress. The latter was a free imitation of sixteenth century Netherlands fashion and was common on the stage. Painters liked to dress their subjects in a way that would emphasize the legendary ("history") or allegoric aspect of the canvas. *The Old Warrior* retains ties with "history" painting, which always remained Rembrandt's main field of endeavour. But as regards the artist's approach to the model, this work already has the essential elements of portraiture: outward likeness, brilliant and painstaking brushwork, a controlled elegance and dignity.

Since 1631, Rembrandt produces commissioned portraits. One of the first is *The Scholar* (1631, Hermitage). It differs from the works typical for the preceding period (such as *The Old Warrior*) primarily in its life-size depiction of the sitter. A viewer's reaction depends on both the scale of a painting and the distance from which it is examined. In a large canvas the general decorative scheme, as well as the approach to the model, must differ from those of a small panel. The young painter understands this perfectly. His compositions acquire a new spaciousness, broad flowing lines encircle large patches of black, white, and gold; the painter's technique becomes more varied, as does the expressive power of his brushwork,—from obscure to strikingly conspicuous strokes. Utilizing the commonly acknowledged formula of the Dutch portrait, Rembrandt introduces many novelties discovered during his "facial expression" experiments. In *The Scholar* he depicts a momentary state: while bent over his desk in writing, something suddenly diverted the scholar's attention, making him turn his head. This is the state of a person startled by the arrival of unheralded visitors or struck by a sudden thought. In all probability the painter realized that this approach would limit his potential. In other portraits of that period he never goes so far in his attempts to seize the fleeting moment, convey a transient state of mind. The one possible exception are some of the figures in his *Anatomy Lesson of Doctor Tulp* (1632, The Hague), a large group portrait of the members of the Amsterdam Guild of Surgeons.

Between 1632 and 1636 Rembrandt, who, by that time, has settled down in Amsterdam, receives quite a number of commissions for portraits. The painter is young and industrious, yet even his inspiration and creative imagination falter before such a torrent of paintings. He knows how to produce very different paintings depending on the client's nature, but he also evolves a series of devices, ready-made formulas, which can be easily applied. A good example, typical of a large group of paintings based on such devices, is his oval *Portrait of a Young Man with a Lace Collar* (1634, Hermitage). The expression of the face with its meaningless, polite smile follows the fashionable stereotype, yet the sitter's general aspect is one of complete ease and freedom, there are no immobile or frozen elements. This feeling is mainly due to the play of light and shade—soft, warm and living. There is little doubt that such a truly "pleasing" painting was much to the liking of the customer: the painter created an image exactly like that which the handsome young dandy would have wished to recognize as his own self. Such paintings established Rembrandt's popularity with the public of Amsterdam.

In his portraits Rembrandt depicts the contemporary scene. But while painting "histories", he draws inspiration from biblical tales or myths and gives free rein to his imagination. In the 1630s these two aspects of his painting become distinctly separated. During this period, however, the artist creates a number of works of intermediary character. They are extremely varied, some of them nearer to plot pictures, others to portraits. Such, on the one hand, are the single-figure paintings where the sitter, in sumptuous dress, appears as an Oriental potentate or general, biblical prophet or wise rabbi; on the other hand, such are the dress self-portraits of the artist or portraits of his friends. To the latter belong his *Portrait of a Boy* (ca. 1633) and *Saskia as Flora* (1634), both in the Hermitage collection.

14

In *Portrait of a Boy* the artistic scheme is secondary to the painstaking brushwork. The painter focuses his attention upon the rich costume and the chiaroscuro technique he has evolved by that period; the latter becomes the dominant recognizable feature of his work: shade envelops the foreground and engulfs the background; in contrast, the face and upper part of the figure, touched by light, stand out with breath-taking vividness. The artist will modify this formula countless times in his painting.

If *Portrait of a Boy* can be regarded as a minor work, *Flora* belongs among Rembrandt's unique and most inspired achievements. It is one of a group of Saskia portraits which occupy a very special place in Rembrandt's creations of the 1630s. The artist feels an insurmountable urge to convey the rare charm he sees in Saskia: hence the intimate, deeply emotional and genuine character of this lovely woman's image. In the Hermitage painting, Saskia-Flora materializes, as it were, from a mysterious gloom; the green bushes, touched with light, and the staff wound around with flowers, not filling the space to the right and left of the figure, emphasize its depth. The painting of the delicate face and hands, of the large bright flowers, of the cape of greenish silk and transparent striped fabric of the sleeves, is of exceptional beauty. Rembrandt conveys the material beauty of the world so completely and powerfully as to leave far behind even the professional still-life painters of the Dutch school.

The portraits of Saskia belong among those works where the artist's aim was to lift the world of painting above the commonplace, beyond the realm of real social relations. Here he drew on his experience in the "history" painting genre, on his ability to convey thoughts through the images of ancient lore. Contrary to many of his contemporaries, reality for him was complex: it was part of a system of poetic associative ideas where fantasy and life blend into one. The image of the flower goddess merges in Rembrandt's mind with that of a living woman. Saskia was beautiful, and she did not need any idealization to pose a goddess.

Notwithstanding the multitude of portraits, "histories" remain the primary feature of Rembrandt's work. His experiments here are of an exceptionally wide range.

At the very beginning of his Amsterdam period, Rembrandt painted a small grisaille, *Adoration of the Magi* (1632, Hermitage). This type of work is a rarity. Some of his grisailles were later used as originals for etchings, this being common practice in the seventeenth century. But this was not his only purpose: grisailles, for him, possessed an artistic expressiveness of their own.

With the exception of a few more or less rough drawings, Rembrandt as a rule made no preliminary sketches. The final version of a painting was created directly on canvas where preparatory stages were buried underneath the last layers of paint. Their traces may be uncovered by X-ray photography, a method which often gives spectacular results when applied to Rembrandt's pictures. All the same, we would have very little idea of the first stages of his work, were it not for his grisailles, which allow some insight into his working process. As far as we can judge, at the initial stage of his work Rembrandt limited himself to white, ochre and lamp-black, and began to paint after having first covered the white priming with wide patches of transparent brown. Hardly touching it in the shaded areas, he "built" the lighted parts of figures with white, outlining them with long strokes of brownish-black. The Hermitage *Adoration of the Magi* is a good example of this technique, though some of the contours and surfaces are done in greater detail. X-ray study reveals many subsequent changes: evidently Rembrandt could not at once solve the composition problems to his full satisfaction. Nevertheless, this painting shows a great "emancipation" of artistic style, a high degree of emotional tension. The unfinished picture betrays the same temperament that the young artist was not able to control a few years earlier in his *Christ Driving the Money-changers from the Temple*. Thus the recent attribution of the *Adoration of the Magi* enriches our collection of the Dutch master's works with a rare and, in many respects, highly noteworthy creation.

A great many pictures bear witness to Rembrandt's variegated artistic search in the field of "history" painting in the 1630s: *The Incredulity of St Thomas* (1634, Pushkin Museum) and four Hermitage paintings, *The Descent from the Cross* (1634), *Abraham's Sacrifice* (1635), *Parable of the Labourers in the Vineyard* (1637), and *Danaë* (1636 and *ca.* 1646).

The Incredulity of St Thomas (1634, Pushkin Museum) embodies a certain artistic formula, as typical for many Rembrandt narrative paintings as the oval *Portrait of a Young Man* (1634, Hermitage) is typical for commissioned portraits of those years.

The theme of sudden divine intervention held the painter's interest throughout his life. The miraculous appearance of Christ risen from the dead or of a heavenly messenger in the guise of an angel plays no small role in Rembrandt's legacy. This interest reflects the artist's religious beliefs, as well as those of his society and times. Their meaning changes from decade to decade, pregnant with a wealth of complex psycho-philosophic associations. *The Incredulity of St Thomas* and *Abraham's Sacrifice*, produced in the 1630s, are examples of a somewhat superficial and illustrative portrayal of a religious subject. *The Incredulity of St Thomas* is suggestive of a theatrical staging. In the centre on a dais we see the resurrected Christ; his shining nimbus serves as the source of light in the central part of the panel, contrasted to the surrounding gloom. The figures grouped around Christ form a boundary line for the light. Dramatic light effects are extremely typical of Rembrandt's painting of that period. The reaction aroused by the miracle is limited, mainly, to various expressions of surprise and curiosity, long included in Rembrandt's artistic repertory. This relatively small painting could not but meet with approval: it told a story, carried a moral message, and, pleasant to the eye, could serve as an interior decoration piece.

The Descent from the Cross from the Hermitage collection was produced in the same year. The subject had a long iconographic tradition in European art. Its supreme representation was thought to be the altar painting by Rubens in the Antwerp cathedral, widely known thanks to Lucas Vorsterman's engraving. Rembrandt's creative thought revolves in the vicinity of this tradition, returning to it while constantly choosing new paths. Very unusual for the preceding development of European art, they are highly typical of Rembrandt's artistic manner—it is not by chance that his *Descent from the Cross* is so reminiscent of *The Incredulity of St Thomas*. Rubens depicted the sublime grief of a group of noble men and women over the death of a noble hero; Rembrandt depicted a nocturnal mass scene full of dramatic tension. The numerous figures dissolve into the darkness, reappear in a ray of light, and the crowd seems to move, to be alive, as it mourns the crucified Christ and pities his mother. The portrayal of the people is in no way idealized: many of them are rough-looking, even ugly. Their emotions are very strong, but these are emotions of ordinary people, not purified by the sublime catharsis inherent in Rubens's painting. The dead Christ is one of them, and only the degree of their sorrow gives his suffering and death a special importance. The meaning of the painting is probably revealed not so much by Christ himself as by the man supporting him and pressing his cheek to Christ's body.

From the viewpoint of artistic perfection, this fractional though tense composition is inferior both to Rubens's famous work and to certain other paintings produced by Rembrandt during that same period. *The Incredulity of St Thomas*, intrinsically a less portent work, possesses a greater external harmony. Yet *The Descent from the Cross* conveys better the deep interpretation of biblical themes that was Rembrandt's.

16

Having made the Scriptures the subject of historical and philological commentary, the humanitarians of the sixteenth and seventeenth centuries developed a fundamentally new approach to them. The age-old tradition of allegorical interpretation, which made the ancient tales conform to religious dogma, becomes the point of heated argument. Protestant theology insists on regarding the Bible as an authentic historical source. Independently of theories, there appears a marked tendency in art (manifested, for instance, in the work of Lucas van Leyden) to convey the literal meaning of biblical narration, as opposed to the symbolic. The possibility to transfer those happenings to reality, to see their participants as concrete people with their own individual inner world, seems attractive to many painters. The first sprouts of such interpretation appear in Holland in the sixteenth century; with the victory of Protestantism in the seventeenth century, it flowers. The Protestant interdiction of prayer to images severs the link between art and the Church. As a result, the religious theme begins to occupy a less important place in Dutch painting, while the choice and interpretation of subjects acquire a greater liberty. The limited scope of subject-matter sanctified by Middle Age tradition is, to a large extent, ignored; painters choose to depict concrete facts instead of great mysteries. However, by far not every painter, if he has lost the possibility to lean on tradition for support, is capable of revealing the supreme meaning of this or that biblical event. A rational understanding of the Scriptures forms the basis of the illustrative, prosaic and genre interpretation of religious subject-matter in Dutch painting. It also opens new vistas to Rembrandt.

Behind the Bible's lapidary style Rembrandt, with his highly imaginative mind, sees an entire and detailed scene full of tense dramatism. *The Descent from the Cross* to him is a convincing portrayal of a real event. The master intended to convey the truth of life itself as he understood it. Thus, under his brush, Christ the Redeemer becomes just a dead man, and the theological sense of the event gives way to the human. Authenticity co-exists with a strong element of premeditated artistic arbitrariness, all the more evident because the predilections of the author bear the imprint of a marked individuality. This can be traced in all aspects of the painting, from its general chiaroscuro structure to the fanciful details of the Oriental costume of one of its personages. The new reading of the Scriptures opened to painters a new area of subject-matter, unheeded before. Rembrandt turns to the Gospel parable of the labourers in the vineyard, depicting its finale—the settling of accounts (1637, Hermitage). This small picture, painted in a rapid manner, resembles his grisaille "sketches". It is quite possible that the painter did it just for his own pleasure, aiming to fix on canvas some interesting thought. The place of action is reminiscent of a Dutch trade office, but it is modified to conform to Rembrandt's notion of the "picturesque", that is, attractive to the eye. This is apparent in his treatment of space: mysterious dark corners, arches and vaults, complex projections of the floor, and the interplay of lighted and shaded walls. The chaotic conglomeration of books and bales, the richly embroidered table-cloth, the cracked and pock-marked wall with the bird-cage, etc.—all this serves to convey the untidy atmosphere of a dwelling-place. Everyday experience and queer fantasy are combined in the group of people with their exaggerated gestures and the exotic touches of their dress. Rembrandt interprets the Gospel story in the light of such dazzling and striking impressions that the viewer is on the verge of completely forgetting the religious sense of the parable (though it remains of primary importance to both the author and his contemporaries). There is nothing accidental in the parallel drawn between the labourers arguing with the master, on the one hand, and the social realities of Holland, on the other; some believe this painting to be the artist's reaction to a definite event—the uprising of the apprentice weavers in his native town of Leyden.

17

Rembrandt's creative mind is wonderfully concrete. This is true not only of such scenes as *The Labourers in the Vineyard*, but even of pictures most fantastic in subject-matter.

A convincing confirmation of this may be found in one of Rembrandt's largest "history" paintings of the 1630s, *Abraham's Sacrifice* (1635, Hermitage). Up to now, we have discussed narrative paintings which occupy a very special place in European art of that time because of both the highly original manner of the artist and the characteristic traits of the Dutch national school. In this painting, however, Rembrandt attempts to rival the famous masters of the Baroque whose solemn and effective altarpieces graced the churches of Catholic countries. His *Abraham*, a large-size canvas with a characteristic decorative composition, may seem to bear resemblance to these altarpieces. But appearances are often misleading, and in effect the difference between Rembrandt's creation and the others is great. A Baroque altar painting must necessarily have monumental pictorial qualities that allow it to play a key role in a church interior as an ornamental and architectural entity. Rembrandt's creation is, notwithstanding its dimensions, first and foremost an easel painting. It is endowed in high measure with illusionism, characteristic of the Dutch school. Here Rembrandt's search in the depiction of passions and intermediary emotional states yields a degree of expressiveness which allows this image to be qualified as classic. Steeped in sorrow, Abraham cannot grasp the fact that deliverance has come; he is stunned, but has not yet had the time to take it in and rejoice. This complex psychological content, visible to the viewer only from a relatively short distance, is one of the achievements of easel painting. An interesting detail—the knife dropped by Abraham in his surprise—will arrest the viewer's attention: the fleet second depicted represents the culmination of action and the moment of supreme emotional stress. The entire picture serves as an illustration of Rembrandt's words concerning his attempts to convey "the greatest and the most natural movement" * (physical and spiritual). To portray physical and emotional culmination is one of the main aims of Baroque art. But Rembrandt's depiction is narrowed to an "instant", which is incompatible with the monumental decorative aims characteristic of this style.

Rembrandt's work proves that he felt quite at home in the art of his times and in the heritage of the sixteenth century, which continued to exert a strong influence on artistic practice. He has many common points with the problems of the Caravaggio and the Baroque schools, in spite of the fact that under his brush the artistic aims and techniques advanced by these two international mainstreams of art take on a completely new look. A fundamentally different understanding of the problems underlies their outward similarity. In *Abraham* Rembrandt's quest goes parallel to that of the masters of Baroque in Flanders and Italy, yet a great difference exists between him and these masters in what concerns the very basis of artistic perception and pictorial representation.

The wonderfully concrete character of Rembrandt's artistic methods reveals his strong ties with the national tradition. At the same time he deliberately opposes his "history" painting to the current of Dutch genre art, striving to set higher standards of creative thought. As a result of this, his art of the 1630s, though firmly bound to definite conditions of time and place, grows into a unique phenomenon of both Dutch and European art of that age. One of its specific traits is an "Oriental" world, created by Rembrandt's imagination; just as Shakespeare transferred his dramas to "Bohemia" or "Illyria", Rembrandt made the "Orient" the setting of his biblical stories.

It is in this strange world of fantasy that we find the heroine of one of his most wonderful and

---

* C. Hofstede de Groot, *Urkunden über Rembrandt*, Den Haag, 1906, Nr 65.

mysterious paintings—the famous *Danaë*. Among the many problems that arise in connection with this canvas, the most important, to our mind, is that of its date; the problem became even more controversial after the X-ray studies which furnished amazing data: the central part of the picture was painted twice, each time in a different manner. The date 1636, accepted until recently, refers to the first version of the painting, while the repainting must be dated somewhere between 1646 and 1647, i.e. a decade later.* It is a commonly known fact that during this period Rembrandt's art underwent profound changes; it suffices to compare *Abraham's Sacrifice* with *The Holy Family with Angels* (1645, Hermitage) to see the vast difference between the master's work of the 1630s and 1640s in such things as technique, artistic aims, and frame of mind. To return to a picture long finished called for a certain amount of courage: the painter must have had weighty reasons, and personal reasons at that, for it seems that neither version of *Danaë* was commissioned.

The situation is somewhat reminiscent of Rembrandt's work on the gigantic group portrait known as *The Night Watch* (1642, Amsterdam). This huge canvas is in many respects the highest point of the artist's search of the 1630s, but its final accomplishment came at a time when those problems were already exhausted and Rembrandt was painting works of a different character.

In the case of *Danaë* we are not dealing with a gradual change of artistic concept over a long period of constant work; we have here a fundamental remaking of a painting long finished. Here it was almost impossible to combine the old with the new, yet Rembrandt solved that problem. True, certain changes were evident to the specialist's eye, but the possibility of two distinctly different stages was not considered until recently. The only doubts concerned the half-obliterated date: 1636 or 1646? Features typical of the 1630s were by far predominant, so the earlier date became the traditionally accepted one, though much spoke against this assumption: the amazing psychological expressiveness of Danaë's hand, the complex play of strong emotions on her face, the striking technique which conveyed with unequalled spontaneity and power the living flesh of her body. It was obvious that a chasm lay between *Danaë* and the other paintings of the 1630s. To explain this difference, specialists were forced to call *Danaë* a rare creative success, the very summit of Rembrandt's art of that decade. Recent studies, however, showed that the untouched areas of the picture, to the contrary, are quite typical of his painting of that period. Probably the first version of *Danaë* had its proper place among works created between 1635 and 1636. It could indeed have been the master's greatest achievement in a group of paintings which included such works as *Abraham's Sacrifice*, *Belshazzar's Feast* (ca. 1635, London), *The Rape of Ganymede* (1635, Dresden), *Self-portrait with Saskia* (1636, Dresden); the latter painting also underwent serious changes long after the first version had been completed. After a new dating of *Danaë* the painter's work of the 1630s takes on a more consistent aspect.

However, serious difficulties stand in the way of placing the final version among works of the next decade. It would seem that the painter never lost his interest in *Danaë* and in the mid-1640s returned to it, trying to breathe new life into the picture. Rembrandt gave, as it were, a new interpretation of the entire painting without changing the background of the first version. Eliminating certain minor details, he preserved the general luxurious context; nor did he renounce the original ambitious aim of rivalling the great masters of the past in a life-size portrayal of a nude woman. The emotional and physical tangibility of the representation acquired a greater power in the final version.

19

---

* See Ю. Кузнецов, *Загадки «Данаи». К истории создания картины Рембрандта*, Ленинград, 1970.

Danaë, with its multiple ties with the period of the 1630s, is rather an exception where creations of the 1640s are concerned. The lack of any real analogies makes the exact dating problematic. But one thing remains true: even though hyper-dynamic movement and emotions disappear from Rembrandt's work, his era of "Sturm und Drang" does not end with *The Night Watch* (1642). His interests of the 1630s are to a great extent determined by the basic traits of his character. The outwardly controlled, inner-looking art of the following decade co-exists with his predilection for luxury and the exotic motifs: it preserves his latent temperamental tension, his openly spontaneous emotions. Studying the main tendencies of Rembrandt's art, we often contrast one period with another; but in reality its continuity is evident throughout, while each separate decade is more variegated than is traditionally believed.

Rembrandt's plot paintings of the 1640s are represented, besides *Danaë*, by two outstanding works: *David's Farewell to Jonathan* (1642) and *The Holy Family with Angels* (1645), both in the Hermitage collection. The first pertains to the beginning of the new decade, but it shows typical signs of the years to come: the combination of intense emotions with outward restraint and concentration. The subject of this painting has been interpreted in different ways, but this is of minor importance compared to the artistic system which the viewer perceives first and foremost. The breath-takingly beautiful combination of delicate colours in the costumes of the characters, rarely found in Rembrandt's work, is in tune with the surrounding greenish gloom that clears in the distance where rises the majestic Temple of Jerusalem. The dazzling beauty of the painting transfers the action to the realm of exalted poetry.

David and Jonathan stands as one of the summits in the development of a theme characteristic of Rembrandt—the sublimated poetic world where man and nature are endowed with supreme spiritual meaning and beauty. It may be said that Rembrandt, while discovering the aesthetic value of commonplace reality, attained a complete and lasting understanding of the dream-world he had discovered long before.

The new sphere of the master's interests found its full realization in his *Holy Family*, painted three years later. Many regard it as a direct illustration of Dutch family life, in agreement with Goethe who said: "Rembrandt copied his Madonna from a Dutch peasant woman." Special emphasis is put on the last three words, in the Goethe tradition, to underline the difference between Rembrandt and other painters who saw in the Madonna an ideal of pure beauty. Indeed, Rembrandt's interpretation of the Gospel is very down-to-earth and democratic. The prerequisites for this can be traced to his paintings of the 1630s, for instance, *The Descent from the Cross* and *The Labourers in the Vineyard*. However, it was only when he turned from the portrayal of dramatic events to that of everyday family life that he was able to fully realize an interpretation of the Gospel through life.

The convincing quality of Rembrandt's work rests only in part on the authentic reflection of reality's outward aspects, something in which his fellow-countrymen reached a high level of mastery. The number of objects he likes to paint is comparatively limited, and though delicate and beautiful, his painting is never restricted to colour and structure depiction. Rembrandt is not satisfied with the "still" life of objects and people which fills the canvases of the best Dutch still-life or genre painters. Moreover, he does not choose to limit his view of objects to the aspect of the commonplace, an approach characteristic of the art of his contemporaries. Rembrandt's attitude lends his paintings a touch of genre art, even when they depict biblical subjects or scenes of Roman history. The exceptionally high level of the pictorial interpretation of life attained in Holland was the soil from which Rembrandt's art had grown, though often he used the exper-

20

ience of his contemporaries only as a spring-board. Thus, if we ignored the small group of angels in his *Holy Family*, we could see the painting as a scene taken from everyday life. But with Rembrandt, contrary to genre painters, the essential thing was a study of human relations. The key figure is Mary: she embodies the meaning of the painting. Rembrandt sees her as a mother, with a mother's love for her child and a mother's simple, everyday troubles. These natural feelings and relations become strangely important under the painter's brush. Descending from heavenly heights to the home of a poor Dutch carpenter, the Virgin Mary assumes new spiritual beauty and grandeur. On the other hand, for the first time in the history of European art were ordinary human feelings and emotions seen and depicted with such vividness and spontaneity. The traditions of artistic thought of the age, as well as Rembrandt's creative credo, excluded the expression of such concepts in the genre-art form. They belonged to the "history" painting sphere. In this case, the nature of the subject permitted a genre treatment, but the artist's problem was typical of his "history" painting. He discovers the supreme spiritual richness, religious and human, in the lives of simple people; the evangelic tale is in his eyes the embodiment of both.

This element of supreme spiritual significance is less obvious in his small *Portrait of an Old Woman with Spectacles* (1643, Hermitage). The face with its rather vacuous expression conveys little more than the model's features. The sumptuous dress speaks of ties with biblical prophetesses and pious wise old women; that is not sufficient, however, to include this painting in the "history" series as Rembrandt understood it. Notwithstanding its outward similarity to Rembrandt's portraits or his "history" paintings, this picture is actually much closer to genre art, and as such constitutes a rarity in Rembrandt's legacy. No wonder that some scholars voiced doubts concerning its authorship and attributed it to one of Rembrandt's pupils.

In the 1640s, there is a marked drop in the number of portraits produced by Rembrandt, though their diversity of manner never lessens. Along with the romantic dress portraits, there exists a group of paintings where such elements as simplicity and restraint are emphasized, much in the tradition of Dutch art. At times, in official commissioned portraits, this restraint is meant to convey a standard of conduct customary among the Dutch patricians. At other times, the man in the picture "lines" naturally and free of constraint, with no thought of impressing the viewer. These paintings, often modest to the eye, can be ranked among the supreme achievements of the master.

The Soviet museums possess two paintings that mark the beginning and end of Rembrandt the portraitist's search along these lines in the 1640s: *Portrait of Baertjen Martens Doomer* (ca. 1640, Hermitage) and *Portrait of an Old Woman* (ca. 1650, Pushkin Museum). Baertjen Martens, far from being a woman of the world, was the wife of an artisan who frequented artistic circles; while working on her portrait, Rembrandt could give free rein to his creative impulses. Using diverse techniques, he conveys the expressive features of his model's mobile face. The starting point here is Rembrandt's masterly drawing, an integral part of his painting. The painter finds something worthy of respect in Baertjen Martens, with her restless, boisterous ways; he aims for complete authenticity, trying to show her exactly as she is.

The dynamic poignancy of the portrait is, of course, connected with the model's nature. Rembrandt's interest in her character can be traced to his preoccupation with "the most natural movement" of which he spoke in the 1630s. Rembrandt's artistic problems of two decades dovetail here and constitute an entity. From *Baertjen Martens*, through several works of the 1640s, we come to the *Portrait of an Old Woman* (ca. 1650, Pushkin Museum).

By this time, a marked similarity appears between commissioned portraits and those that the artist paints for himself. In the first, the approach toward the model is based increasingly on

21

human, as opposed to social, criteria; the second become simple and unassuming. The element of dual *Weltanschauung*, typical of the 1630s (though Rembrandt was probably not conscious of it), disappears. This, in turn, may be traced to the painter's different approach toward commissioned portraits and "histories".

The long, gradual process of the "crystallization" of a comprehensive method at times gives paintings that combine the characteristic traits of commissioned and non-commissioned portraits. Toward the end of the 1640s the appearance of such pictures becomes a kind of regular phenomenon. An example of this is the *Portrait of an Old Woman*. The broad red shawl covering the model's head (a detail Rembrandt liked very much), strange to the dress of that period, and the old-fashioned "Burgundy" costume, make one presume, albeit with hesitation, that this was not a commissioned portrait. Yet its scrupulous objectivity allows it to be placed together with the commissioned works of the preceding years. This canvas, with its multifaceted psychological characterization and its grandiose composition, based on large splashes of colour, lies at the source of one of Rembrandt's main portrait tendencies of the 1650s. We speak here about the uncommissioned portraits of old men and women, of his own family or other models.

Important prerequisites of further development are evident in another group of paintings of the 1640s, represented by *Portrait of an Old Man* (ca. 1643—45, Hermitage). The frankly ugly face with its flabby, shapeless features betrays a passive, hopeless acceptance of the hardships of life. The man's character makes itself felt through the emotional state that grips him. In contrast to certain portraits of the early 1630s (*Portrait of a Scholar*, 1631; *The Anatomy Lesson of Doctor Tulp*, 1632), this tense emotional state is in no way connected with the surroundings: it stems from the man's nature, thus characterizing him to the full. The approach and solution here are more one-sided, more subjective than in paintings of the *Baertjen Martens* or *Portrait of an Old Woman* type; this portrait has more in common with the emotional characterization of the personages in Rembrandt's narrative paintings.

"Man and his emotional state"—one might thus define the main problem of Rembrandt's art. A source of constant interest to the painter, it is evident, in one form or another, in all of his canvases, but acquires special emphasis in his works of the 1650s and 1660s.

In the 1650s the portrait plays an exceptionally important role in Rembrandt's art. Soviet museums possess several outstanding portraits of that period. Five canvases constitute a more or less single whole: these are uncommissioned portraits of old people, produced around 1654. It is fascinating to follow the painter's different approach to the solution of a similar problem in each of these portraits.

The most impressive of all is *Portrait of an Old Man in Red* (ca. 1652—54, Hermitage), which probably preceded the rest. Possessing a very high degree of generalization, the portrait also conveys the individual build of the old man, hints at the way he carries himself, etc. His pose is almost symmetrical in its rock-like immobility; the symmetry is slightly disturbed by the position of the face and hands, and especially by the man's gaze, which seems to follow the direction of the light. Avoiding the viewer's eyes, he appears to alienate himself from witnesses.

The portrayal of people "alone with themselves" is a common feature of Rembrandt's later works. A state of deep meditation and concentration is best suited for revealing man's inner world in all its complexity. The presupposed "solitude" of the model is a manifestation of the painter's rich experience in life and art, of his imagination and intuition. In reality the sitter, being in the constant presence of the painter, can but rarely divert his thoughts from the fact that he is exhibiting himself, through the painter's medium, to future viewers.

Treating only a "fleeting moment" in the flow of life,—something that all painters do,—Rembrandt never checks that flow. The viewer reads, as it were, the different thoughts and emotions that fleet across the face of the old man, lost in deep meditation. What is more, the painting conveys a sense of the specific rhythm of the sitter's life, and in each new work the rhythm is modified. One cannot but think of Shakespeare's somewhat ironic words: "Time travels in divers paces with divers persons" (*As You Like It*, Act III, Scene 2). But in the works of both Shakespeare and Rembrandt the "pace of time" is subject to much more complex metamorphoses than those mentioned by Shakespeare ("I'll tell you who Time ambles withal, who Time trots withal, who Time gallops withal, and who he stands still withal"), all depending on the emotional situation and the character of the person portrayed.

Rembrandt's subtle understanding of human nature and his deep penetration into the dialectics of man's inner life not only determine the structure of every painting of his, but lead him to return again and again to the portrayal of one and the same model. As we know, his *Old Man in an Armchair* (1652, London) portrays the same person as *Old Man in Red*. There exist four portraits of another old man, believed to be, but not without doubts, Adriaen van Rijn, the painter's elder brother (paintings in Berlin, Paris, The Hague and Moscow). In the case of Rembrandt, series of portraits depicting the same model are not due to circumstances (as, for instance, are the Van Dyck portraits of Charles I or those of Philip IV by Velázquez), but come as the result of the painter's deliberate intent.

The Adriaen van Rijn portraits are of great interest to a student of Rembrandt's creative method. The earliest of them (1650, The Hague) reflects the calmest mood of all; here the peculiar traits of the model are shown with strict objectivity. In the next (*Man with a Golden Helmet*, Berlin) the dominant theme is reticence and estrangement. Finally, in the Moscow painting, dated 1654, the model is once again shown in a calm state of meditation, though tinged with bitterness. The free style of painting emphasizes the model's actual emotional and physical state. Underneath the seeming simplicity of the Moscow *Portrait of Adriaen van Rijn* lies a host of spiritual possibilities, as yet untold and obscure. This portrait can hardly be regarded as marking the end of a series.

On the other hand, in the three other portraits of 1654 the models "speak" for themselves eloquently. The Hermitage *Portrait of an Old Woman* and *Portrait of an Old Jew* are probably companion portraits. They complement each other, more by contrast than by similarity.

The *Old Jew* is remarkable for its dramatic tension. The man, bent over with age, leans forward watchfully; the real-life rhythm of this characteristic movement determines the counterpoise of volumes and splashes of light which forms the basis of the picture. Light sharpens the large, clear-cut features of the man's face, with its pronounced message of bitterness, indignation and readiness to withstand the onslaughts of both men and fate. Strong feelings completely rule this man, constituting the essence of his inner world, of his individuality. A different model leads the painter along a different path: in the case of his *Old Man in Red*, for instance, emotions ruled by thought become part of an outlook which may be called philosophical.

Emotion is also clearly read in his *Portrait of an Old Woman* (1654, Hermitage). The sorrowful turn of the head, the stooping figure of the old woman were certainly copied from nature. The dominant mood of passive, hopeless reconciliation with the incomprehensible cruelty of life is characteristic of several of Rembrandt's later paintings.

The same woman evidently sat for the Moscow *Portrait of an Old Woman*, also dated 1654. Here one can see the next stage in the painter's interpretation of the model's individuality. From

23

the portrayal of a concrete state of mind, no matter how typical, the painter turns to a generalization of the human condition and human fate as an indissoluble whole. Looking away from concrete circumstances of everyday life, he depicts a human being "face to face with eternity". The Moscow *Portrait of an Old Woman* is an outstanding example of Rembrandt the portraitist's credo, for it embodies the entire system of his artistic views and methods. The centrepoint of the painting is the face; all other elements are subordinate to it. The layers of paint are applied with extremely varied techniques; around the eyes and in the shaded areas of the face there is an interplay of semitransparent dabs and patches of colour, in the lighted areas, a layer of impasto. The characteristic technique here is the constant change of colour in each of the painter's open strokes. This is apparent above all on the borderline of light and shade. Applying broad multicoloured strokes, Rembrandt divides the form into diversely coloured planes occupying different positions in space, the final result being the effect of volume. Versions of this principle are known to every great painter, but it is only rarely that one comes across a work of art in which it is realized as completely as in Rembrandt's mature paintings.

The constructive artistic language is fraught with a world of associations. The content of the portrait acquires rare dimensions: the model becomes imbued, as it were, with all his or her past spiritual history, since every man's nature is conditioned by his past, by the entire life he has lived. The evolution of this "biographical" type of portrait went parallel with the solution of several other problems, first and foremost that of the basic attitude towards the world. The old men and women of the 1654 portraits possess a deeply tragic outlook; they know life to be full of sorrow, cruelty and injustice. They find this outlook to be the only possible one, since it represents a conclusion reached long ago, the result of their life experience.

While seeming to depict people in an isolated state, Rembrandt actually exposes their complex ties with life. Rembrandt's old men and women are interpreted as the embodiment of human wisdom; their judgement of life is naturally assumed to be a supreme truth. These personages stand at the summit of European seventeenth century art and have no direct heirs. Only in the nineteenth century would artists face a problem similar to Rembrandt's, and that would be when democratic culture gave the image of the people a totally new character.

In the pictures just discussed, the painter, as it were, set himself the task of penetrating the model's character while drawing extensive generalizations. But during his entire creative life, including the later period, he continues to produce portraits where his primary interest is not so much individuality as emotions, a particular state of mind. *Portrait of a Man* (1661, Hermitage) is a case in point. The sitter's outward appearance, with his big beard and "Burgundy" dress, is singular; singular, too, is the facial expression: the model is the very embodiment of grief. Certainly, this was no whim of Rembrandt's; seizing on what he saw as the dominating aspect of the man's outlook, he swamped all other emotions in this single one. When evaluating such works, one must keep in mind that to Rembrandt half-length pictures were not necessarily portraits. In many of his later and most significant works, not to mention his early studies of "passions", he did not strive for a portrait-like characterization of the model. Emotionless depiction is as unthinkable to Rembrandt as the depiction of abstract emotion deprived of individuality. Every portrayal has a measure of individual character, yet it is not always a portrait and therefore demands a different evaluation.

Finally, among the last of Rembrandt's works we find the portrait of his friend, the poet Jeremias de Decker (1666, Hermitage). In this case, the image is deprived of any definite emotion. Simultaneously absent-minded and self-absorbed, the sitter lives a life of contemplation before

24

the eyes of the working painter. The portrait belongs to a group of later canvases in which Rembrandt turned to the generally accepted, the most simple and neutral, composition schemes. In his youth he was attracted by striking gestures, by peculiar facial expressions, in other words, by outward manifestations of originality, held in such high esteem by his contemporaries. Now he no longer needs such things; more than that, they would have marred the integrity of his intention, unduly emphasizing one of the elements of his creative idiom. That idiom reaches at times unequalled virtuosity. Thus, the brushwork of de Decker's face is a combination of the simplest of techniques with the most complex interlacing of thick, semitransparent and transparent strokes. Such inimitable painting could appear only as the result of a gigantic creative experience. All its elements are absolutely inseparable, as are its aesthetic aspect and psychological expressiveness. Not one splash of colour, not one dab is of self-sufficing importance; every element carries a message. Hence the impossibility of singling out the psychological aspect of the picture and finding adequate words for it: this aspect is an integral part of the painting.

Rembrandt's "histories" of the fifties and sixties undergo a similar change. They assume portrait-like characteristics, the majority being compositions with half-length figures, devoid of outward action. Their personages, akin to Rembrandt's portrait models, are engrossed in their thoughts and emotions. The Soviet museums possess several pictures of Rembrandt's last period. Three of them are true masterpieces; two others, produced in the 1650s, are more of an interesting than significant nature. One is *Young Woman with Earrings* (1654, Hermitage). This is a rare example of genre art in Rembrandt's legacy. It pictures a woman admiring her finery. Rembrandt is known to have been a passionate collector of beautiful and rare objects; in his self-portraits he often appears dressed in brocade and velvet, wearing furs and precious stones. Here, too, the painter's horizon and intellectual level make themselves felt: the woman's joy is not just simple or naive; one is inclined to seek a deeper and more significant meaning in the painting than the obvious one. In other words, Rembrandt's genre art is perceived as a "history". It is not by chance that this picture is often interpreted as an allegory of vanity, much in holding with the emblematic style of seventeenth century art.

The small and rather singular painting *Christ and the Woman of Samaria* (1659, Hermitage), even in its original condition, could hardly have furnished an adequate idea of "histories" of the 1650s. Now, when the painting is so damaged, one can only get a notion of the master's search in the field of composition: he divides the picture into three parts and creates his own version of the medieval compositional scheme in the form of a triad.

The "history" paintings of the 1660s are represented in Soviet museums by three canvases: *Ahasuerus, Haman and Esther* (1660, Pushkin Museum), *David and Uriah* (?) (ca. 1665) and *The Return of the Prodigal Son* (ca. 1663), both in the Hermitage collection. These paintings permit one to form a judgement of Rembrandt's art of that period, his interests, possibilities and achievements. The last named picture is the supreme accomplishment of the master's late period.

The Moscow *Ahasuerus, Haman and Esther* was painted at the very beginning of the decade. It belongs to Rembrandt's most significant works. It is one of his most quiet, most "silent" paintings: Esther has just voiced her accusation, but the King is steeped in silent thought, undecided whether to believe her or not. The pause, the isolated state of each protagonist give the artist greater possibilities of revealing the character and destiny of each one, as well as their mutual relationship. Man and his inner world, man and his fate—this problem, and its solution, was central to Rembrandt's portraits; it remains so in his "history" paintings of the later period, connected as they are with biblical events.

In *David and Uriah* the "history" painting tendencies of the 1660s are especially evident. The close-up half-length figures against a dark background, the intense emotions of each personage, even the absence of details pointing to some definite biblical episode (which resulted in different interpretations of the subject) — all this is characteristic of Rembrandt's late period.* The messages and relationships of the protagonists are clear: an Oriental noble aware that he is fated to die; a King sending him to his death—not in anger, but in sorrow; an old man, a prophet or sage, looking on with bitterness.

The magnificent *Return of the Prodigal Son* can be considered in some respects to be the crowning achievement of Rembrandt's search,—a search for the human, living meaning of a biblical legend, for the supreme meaning of man's life. The meeting of the father and son, after all their sufferings, is the summing-up, as it were, of their earthly existence. Man is the creation of his own past, and the moment of meeting is so pregnant with it that reconciliated sorrow, regret and repentance take the place of joy. These three paintings were produced in different years, but during the same decade. They vary in size, composition and technique. The participants of Esther's feast are surrounded by vacant space; in *David and Uriah* the figures fill the surface of the canvas,—there is practically no difference between the foreground and background; in the multifigured *Return of the Prodigal Son* the setting is reminiscent of a stage decoration, although it does not play an active role. In the two later pictures, the aesthetic expressiveness of objects is less pronounced than in the first one, where a strong accent was placed, for instance, on Esther's shining gold robe. This enumeration of the differences in the three canvases could be continued, but it is more important to turn our attention to their common features. These features are, at the same time, characteristic of Rembrandt's late painting, which they affected in different degree.

It is often said of Rembrandt's last works that his subjects live "regardless of time and space". This is true only in the sense that they exist regardless of everyday space, cluttered with objects, and everyday time, filled with commonplace events. Their life throbs to a different rhythm. There was a time when the artist found satisfaction in the creation of an imagined Oriental setting. Now, he contents himself with painting the subject's fantastic dress. All other indications of time and surroundings are either absent (*David and Uriah*) or very scarce—a Roman portal, hardly distinguishable in the dark background of the *Prodigal Son*; a table, a pitcher, a plate with two apples on it, and a glass in Haman's hand—such are the attributes of Esther's feast. This sort of restraint is not required by the subject-matter. On the contrary, the two latter scenes could be rich in details; in *The Return of the Prodigal Son* the painter even ignores details mentioned in the Scriptures and included in iconographic tradition (the luxurious dress brought to the returned son and the fatted calf killed in his honour).

The obscure space around the figures serves to weaken the painting's concrete aspect and to strengthen the feeling of significance with which each protagonist and the scene as a whole are endowed. In works of the 1630s this feeling was conveyed, in part, by unusual, resplendent settings. In works of the 1640s, as *The Holy Family*, lofty human feelings were expressed through everyday life episodes. Now, in the late "histories", the spiritual essence of each personage becomes so intense and meaningful that it excludes all mechanical, arbitrary elements of everyday life. There are no ties between the depicted scene and the commonplace happenings, not because of a fantastic entourage, but because here life itself flows on a supreme spiritual level. In this

26

* J. Białostocki, «Ikonographische Forschungen zu Rembrandts Werk», *Münchner Jahrbuch der bildenden Kunst,* VIII, 1957, S. 195—210.

sense it may be said that the principles underlying Rembrandt's "histories" reached their full development in his late works.

Space in Rembrandt's late works has been called "emotional space".* It would be equally right to call his time "emotional". Time is, in a sense, "condensed" for the prodigal son and his father, their entire past being focused on the present moment; yet time continues its smooth and measured flow for the silent and immobile witnesses of this meeting. Time has stopped, run out on Uriah; still alive, he knows that he is as good as dead. The rhythm of emotion is also the rhythm of life, it is the step of fate for all the personages of Rembrandt's paintings. These nuances, difficult to express through words, without doubt affect the viewer's reaction.

Rembrandt's figures merge with the dark space, as though swallowed by it, then in contrast they stand out from it in dazzling array. They exist in an isolated state, surrounded by murky gloom. They remain in this self-absorbed state. Sometimes it seems that they do not notice each other, though unbreakable ties link their fates and lives. All the greater is the emotional effect of the unity of two men who have at last found each other in this world of solitude. The return of the prodigal son becomes a triumph of spiritual unification.

Rembrandt's personages are, as a rule, passive figures. Even Esther serves only as the tool of her people's deliverance, according to the will of God and Mordecai. Delicate and beautiful, she fulfills her message with a modest dignity. In Rembrandt's late art, man's life is bound to fate, in the painter's belief something both inherent in man's nature and existing independently from it. One can be reconciled to one's fate or resist it internally, as we see in his portraits of the 1650s, but to struggle against it is hopeless. The idea of an unavoidable law,—be it the Calvinistic teaching of predetermination or Spinoza's concept of the law of human nature that each man must learn to know and conform to,—was common to Dutch seventeenth century culture. In Rembrandt's case we have neither one nor the other, although his concept of fate is certainly connected with the notion of God's will, on the one hand, and with his own gigantic experience in the artistic comprehension of individual psyche, on the other.

Throughout his work Rembrandt sought to see living people in the protagonists of his "histories": a vivid example is his *Danaë*. However, in the system of abstractions that dominates his pictures of the 1660s, there is no need to stress the individual features of every character. Refuting the secondary and arbitrary, the painter seeks to convey the internal "law" of human nature that governs man's role in the depicted drama. Using literary terms, we could qualify the typical Rembrandt drama as the drama of emotional states and the drama of fate. Its comparison to the drama of characters would seem, as in the case of Shakespeare, a modernization. Finally, any comparison with action drama is obviously out of the question, as all action or physical movement are practically absent from Rembrandt's paintings. The protagonists' deeds remain "off stage"; the main event is either yet to come (*Ahasuerus, Haman and Esther*) or has come to pass (*David and Uriah, The Return of the Prodigal Son*). As we mentioned earlier, the participants' state of mind is not one of expectation or passionate emotion, but is rather a reflection of both man's nature and fate. And the situation in the painting, although dramatically tense, loses some of its self-sufficing significance, while becoming part of Time's continuous flow.

Such a treatment of biblical subjects differs greatly from the somewhat illustrative approach apparent in Rembrandt's early "histories". Now the painter changes at will the character and meaning of the biblical episodes. From a scene of struggle and exultation, Esther's feast becomes a scene

27

* L. Münz, «Rembrandts Alterstil und die Barokklassik», *Jahrbuch der kunsthistorischen Sammlungen in Wien*, N. F., IX, 1935, S. 198.

of passive contemplation. The joyful return of the prodigal son (an allegory of the final reconciliation of God and the sinner) conveys a variety of moods, in which sorrow is the dominating one. In the case of *David and Uriah*, the painting's relation to a particular biblical episode can be questioned: in fact, we may say that Rembrandt illustrates not so much the biblical story as a new and different tale. It can be related to the canonical text in the same way as Shakespeare's tragedy is related to the medieval chronicle of Hamlet, Prince of Denmark. Using the Bible as a spring-board, Rembrandt creates his own plots, he paints his own tragedies of the prodigal son, of Esther and Haman, of the death of Uriah. Typically enough, under Rembrandt's brush every theme assumes an element of tragedy. The canvases of the 1650s already testify to the aged painter's tragic outlook on life; the "histories" of the 1660s betray the same attitude.

The tragic character of Rembrandt's last period is generally explained by his own sad fate and the painful sense of isolation occasionally betrayed in his self-portraits. This certainly played an important part in the painter's work, so dependent on spontaneous and subjective emotions. His art was likewise deeply affected, albeit not directly, by Holland's social reality and certain changes in the spiritual climate, apparent in Dutch artistic culture of the mid-seventeenth century.

In his paintings, however, people and their fates have no direct ties with Dutch social reality. Having gone through a stage of a more concrete (but never purely genre) depiction of reality, Rembrandt comes to vast generalizations. Three centuries later, they continue to ring with authentic truth. They are all the more convincing because we seem to hear the artist's voice. Rembrandt's nature, his thoughts and emotions overwhelm us. It is said that every picture characterizes its author and, in a sense, is his self-portrait. Applied to Rembrandt, this is doubly true.

It now remains to evaluate the collection of Rembrandt's paintings in the Soviet Union as a whole. These 30 pictures represent but a small part of the enormous heritage of a man whose creative path was one of impetuous development, intense and varied search. No museum, no exhibition, however comprehensive they might be, can hope to exhaust his legacy. Naturally, some of the fields of his endeavour are not reflected in our collections. His group portraits are to be found only in Holland; they are few, but occupy a very important place in his heritage. We have no landscapes either, although at a certain time they played no small role in his art. Perhaps the most to be deplored is the absence of self-portraits. Rembrandt produced them throughout his life, sometimes using them as an outlet for his emotions, sometimes as a means of better understanding himself as an artist and a man.

All the same, the Rembrandt collection in Soviet museums gives a very broad and true picture of the master's art. He can be seen here in his development, and the main and most important tendencies of each period can be traced. Official, commissioned portraits and "poetic" dress portraits of different years show the scope of Rembrandt the portraitist. His "history" paintings are represented in just as varied a way—from the first independent steps to the last impressive creations. Among these are some of his supreme achievements. No monograph on Rembrandt ignores such significant works as *Danaë*, *The Holy Family*, *The Return of the Prodigal Son*, paintings that will continue to serve as food for thought to all those interested in the history of European culture. Rembrandt's creative endeavour has no analogies either in painting or in philosophy or literature. The comparison of Rembrandt with Shakespeare and Spinoza, Rubens and Velázquez, Pascal and Leibniz, with his contemporaries, forebears and descendants, helps to understand the unique originality of his method and his true place in our spiritual heritage.

X. Yegorova

PLATES

1. CHRIST DRIVING THE MONEY-CHANGERS FROM THE TEMPLE. 1626

2. THE OLD WARRIOR. 1629—30

3. PORTRAIT OF A SCHOLAR. 1631

5. PORTRAIT OF A BOY. 1633

6. PORTRAIT OF A YOUNG MAN WITH A LACE COLLAR. 1634

1. CHRIST DRIVING THE MONEY-CHANGERS FROM THE TEMPLE. 1626

2. THE OLD WARRIOR. 1629—30

3. PORTRAIT OF A SCHOLAR. 1631

4. THE ADORATION OF THE MAGI. 1632

7. SASKIA AS FLORA. 1634

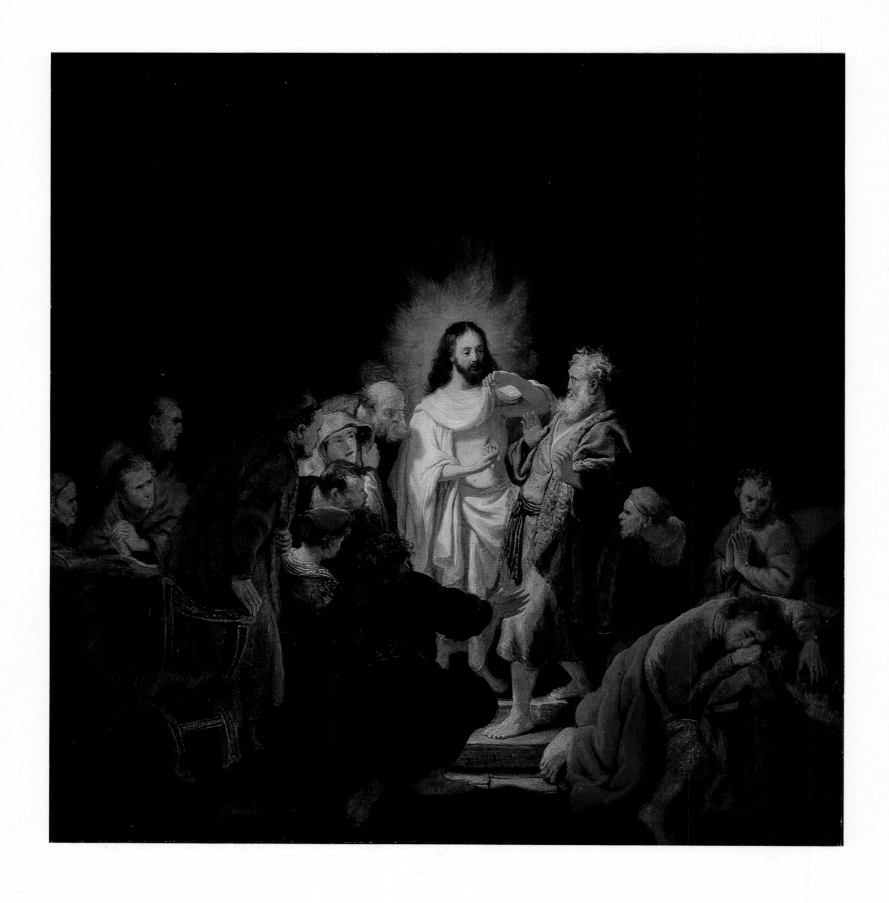

8. THE INCREDULITY OF ST THOMAS. 1634

9. THE DESCENT FROM THE CROSS. 1634

10. ABRAHAM'S SACRIFICE. 1635

11. PARABLE OF THE LABOURERS IN THE VINEYARD. 1637

12. PORTRAIT OF BAERTJEN MARTENS DOOMER. *Ca.* 1640

13. DAVID'S FAREWELL TO JONATHAN. 1642

14. PORTRAIT OF AN OLD MAN. *Ca.* 1643

15. THE HOLY FAMILY WITH ANGELS. 1645

16. PORTRAIT OF AN OLD WOMAN WITH SPECTACLES. 1643

17. DANAË. 1636, 1646—47

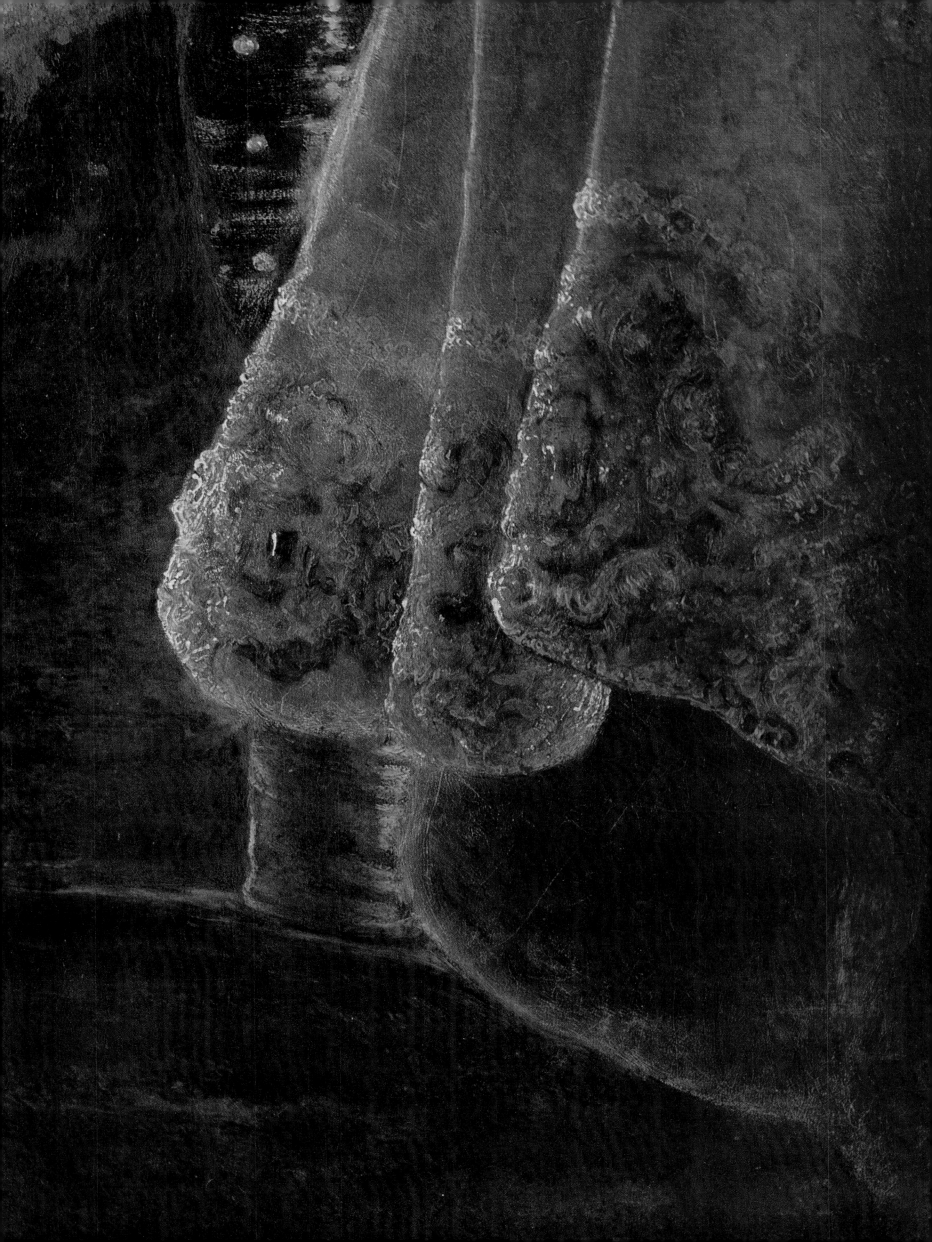

18. PORTRAIT OF AN OLD WOMAN. *Ca.* 1650—52

19. PORTRAIT OF AN OLD MAN IN RED. *Ca.* 1652—54

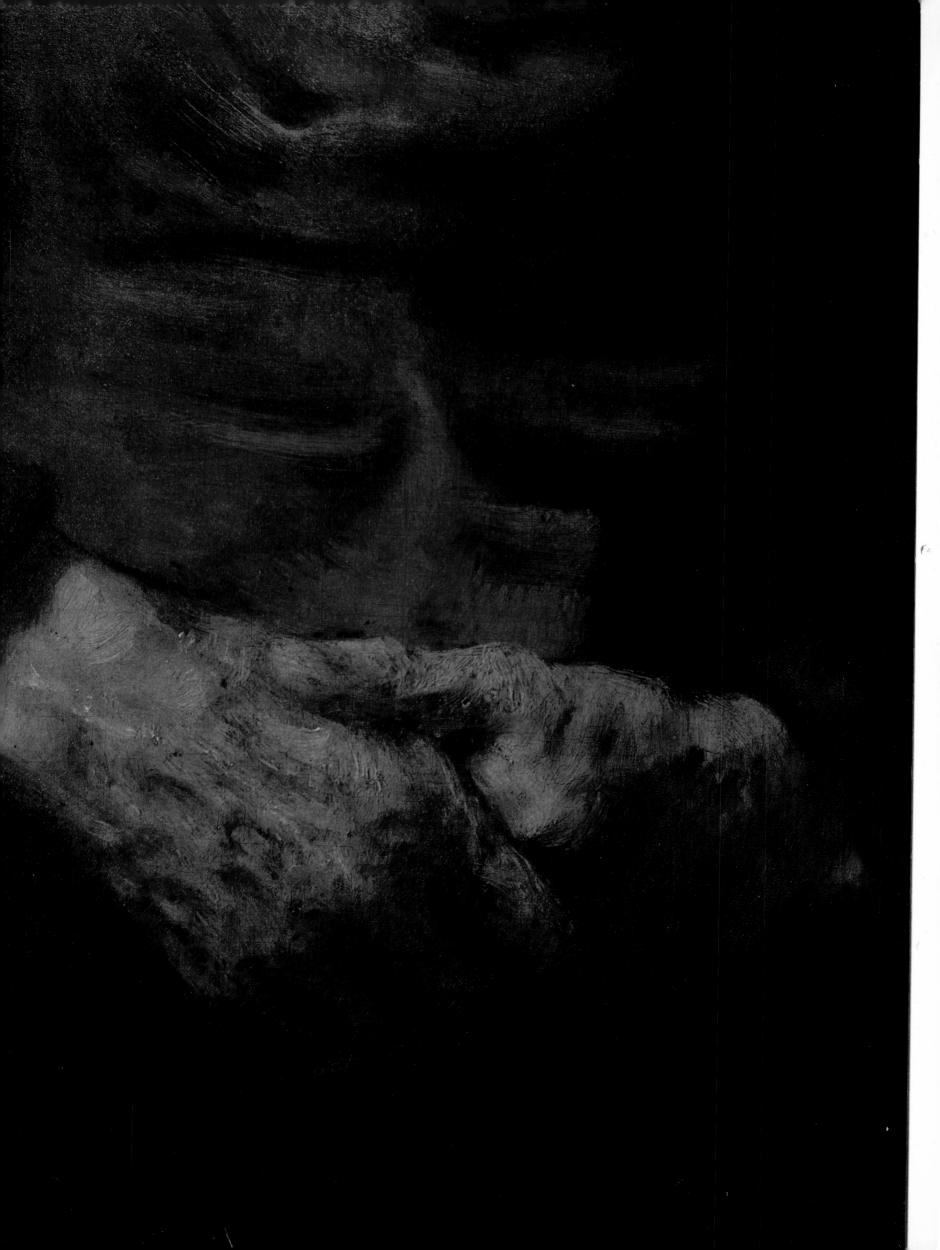

20. PORTRAIT OF ADRIAEN VAN RIJN, REMBRANDT'S BROTHER (?). 1654

21. PORTRAIT OF AN OLD WOMAN. 1654

22. PORTRAIT OF AN OLD JEW. 1654

23. PORTRAIT OF AN OLD WOMAN. 1654

24. YOUNG WOMAN WITH EARRINGS. 1657

25. CHRIST AND THE WOMAN OF SAMARIA. 1659

26. AHASUERUS, HAMAN AND ESTHER. 1660

27. PORTRAIT OF A MAN. 1661

28. THE RETURN OF THE PRODIGAL SON. *Ca.* 1663

29. DAVID AND URIAH (?) [HAMAN ORDERED TO HONOUR MORDECAI (?)]. 1665

30. PORTRAIT OF THE POET JEREMIAS DE DECKER. 1666

Christ Driving the Money-changers from the Temple.
1635. Etching

1. CHRIST DRIVING THE MONEY-CHANGERS FROM THE TEMPLE

Oil on oak, cradled. 43 × 33 cm
Signed with a monogram and dated right of centre (top part of the picture), on the wall:
R. F. 1626
The Pushkin Museum of Fine Arts, Moscow. No 1900

The subject is Christ driving the money-changers from the temple of Jerusalem, for they made his Father's house "a house of merchandise" (*John*, 2. 16). Can religion co-exist with man's desire for personal wealth? This question, one of the most argued during the Reformation period, continued to interest people in the seventeenth century. The evangelic scene painted by Rembrandt gives a clearly negative answer, thus contradicting the mode of life in the burgher republic.

In 1915, when the painting was first mentioned in literature, it was attributed to Rembrandt's school or circle. Similar early works of the painter were not as yet known, with the exception of *The Prophet of Balaam* (now in the Cognacq-Jay Museum, Paris). This latter picture had much in common with the Moscow painting in the structure of faces and figures, the folds of the clothing, the movement of the lifted arms and clasped fists. Yet the attribution of *Balaam* to Rembrandt was not as yet universally conceded. Later Igor Grabar suggested that *Christ Driving the Money-changers from the Temple* was an imitation, which seems highly improbable. In 1924 K. Bauch attributed the painting to Rembrandt. This attribution was corroborated by restoration done in The Hague by Schuring in 1930—31; a detailed report was published by V. Bloch in 1933. The panel, all four sides of which had been added to and measured 53.2 by 40.8 cm, was returned to the original dimensions. The picture was cleaned of a thick dirty

Christ Driving the Money-changers from the Temple.
Detail (X-ray photograph). The Pushkin Museum of Fine Arts, Moscow

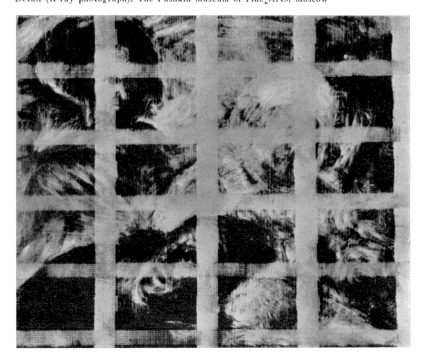

layer of varnish and overpaintings, and it became possible to see the original colour scheme, based on counterpoised dabs of light colour and remindful of Pieter Lastman, Rembrandt's teacher. Finally, there emerged the monogram *R. F.* (*Rembrandt Fecit*), rather unusual for Rembrandt, along with the date *1626*. These facts made the Moscow painting one of the most important in the constantly growing number of analogous works of the period.

However, laboratory examination carried out in 1954 in the Central Restoration Shops of Moscow showed the monogram and date to have been traced in old, dark varnish, not in paint. The control examination in 1962 furnished the same results. This led to the conclusion that the monogram was a falsification: in the process of cleaning, some dirty varnish might have been deliberately left on the picture in such a way as to form the necessary letters and numerals. This hypothesis led Grabar to refute the authenticity of not only the monogram, but of the entire painting. Certain scholars of the older generation (B. Vipper, G. Knuttel), though not admitting it to be a recent imitation, were still doubtful as to whether to attribute it to Rembrandt; they held this view concerning other similar paintings of the same group. Their argumentation was of an aesthetic nature: the painting showed faulty draughtsmanship, was too motley in coloration, too rough in brush-stroke to be considered the work of a great painter. After the War of 1941—45, interest in Rembrandt's first period reaches a new height. A wealth of publications analyse the master's characteristic traits, merits and shortcomings. Both the former and latter are highly evident in the Moscow *Christ Driving the Money-changers from the Temple*. Professional faults are countered with emotional expressiveness, eclectic elements with great originality. The crowded composition is lacking in harmony, but powerfully conveys the fear and surprise of the merchants. Very typical of this group of paintings is the portrayal of Christ — here the artist used as a model Dürer's engraving on the same subject (the series of *Small Passions*). After Dürer, towards the end of the sixteenth century, Dutch engravers repeated this theme: theirs may have been the works that Rembrandt copied. Later, he repeated this figure in an etching dated 1635 (Bartsch 69), where the driving out of the money-changers becomes a turbulent mass scene which abounds in striking details.

In the painting, the brush-strokes do not always follow the form as professional habit demanded, yet they convey the painter's nervous tension and excitement. X-ray investigation shows the rough, impetuous, expressive stroke of the underpaint containing white lead. It also confirms the supposition that we are dealing with the work of a beginning, as yet inexperienced, painter, though of a very independent and original nature. This is certainly not the hesitating hand

Christ Driving the Money-changers from the Temple.
Detail (skew-ray photograph). The Pushkin Museum of Fine Arts, Moscow

of an imitator. Today we may consider the attribution of this canvas to the young Rembrandt's brush as universally accepted.

New studies, carried out in May, 1970, showed the painting to have suffered considerably. Ultraviolet photography reveals traces of overpainting and spots of varnish on Christ's beard and left forearm, in the upper left-hand corner, to the left of the bearded money-changer's profile in the lower part of the painting, and along its lower edge. Scratches in the wet paint, a technique favoured by the young Rembrandt, are in abundance. The monogram and date are in convex impasto — hence the dirty varnish that remained in the convexities after cleaning. In two or three places there are traces of blackish colour under the strips of varnish. The convexities have no clear-cut contour, as in the case of the author's scrapings in wet paint; evidently they were impressed when the coat had begun to dry. This dates back to the painting's creation, not to recent times: the paint has hardened greatly over a three-century period. In short, the monogram must be acknowledged as authentic, although in the process of cleaning efforts were applied to make the inscription stand out.

PROVENANCE:

Before 1915 P. Giraud Collection, Moscow
1924 The Pushkin Museum of Fine Arts, Moscow

EXHIBITIONS:

1915 Paintings of Old Western European Masters from Private Collections. Moscow (Cat., p. 30, No 181)
1936 Rembrandt. Moscow—Leningrad (Cat., p. 43, No 1)
1956 Rembrandt and His School. Moscow—Leningrad (Cat., p. 63)
1969 Rembrandt. Moscow (Cat., pp. 12—13, 15, No 1)

LITERATURE:

В. Щавинский, «Нидерландские мастера в московских частных собраниях», *Старые годы*, 1915, июль—август, с. 111—112, воспр. с. 108; K. Bauch, «Zur Kenntnis von Rembrandts Frühwerken», *Jahrbuch der preußischen Kunstsammlungen*, XLV, 1924, S. 277—280; Weisbach 1926, S. 118; Bauch 1933, S. 11—13, 173; V. Bloch, «Zum frühen Rembrandt», *Oud-Holland*, 1933, blz. 97—100; Benesch 1935, S. 2; Hamann 1948, S. 197, 199, 258; H. E. van Gelder, *Rembrandt en de Heilige Schrift*, Amsterdam [195...], blz. 4, 10; G. Knuttel, "Rembrandt's Earliest Works", *The Burlington Magazine*, XC, 1955, pp. 259—260; Левинсон-Лессинг 1956, с. V, табл. 1; Виппер 1957, с. 277, 328 (прим. 194); Bauch 1960, S. 110—112; Каталог ГМИИ 1961, с. 156; V. Bloch, "A Return to Russia", *Apollo*, LXXX, 1964, p. 292; Фехнер 1965, № 1, с. 34—37; Bauch 1966, Nr 42; Gerson 1968, pp. 13, 24, 488, No 5; Bredius, No 532; Исследование картин Рембрандта, с. 389—395.

2. THE OLD WARRIOR

Oil on oak, cradled. 36 × 26 cm. The panel is octagonal.
Signed with a monogram on the background, right: *RHL*
The Hermitage, Leningrad. No 756

The old man, depicted here in the apparel of a soldier, is to be often encountered in the painter's early works. He first sat for Rembrandt in 1626 as the old money-changer in *Christ Driving the Money-changers from the Temple* (see No 1), then as *St Peter* (Fine Arts Museum, Boston, Bredius 73), then as a warrior in fantastic dress (Brian Mountain Collection, London, Bredius 79; Art Institute of Chicago, Bredius 81). His face may also be recognized in a portrait study, one of a series painted in those years (Mauritshuis Royal Picture Gallery, The Hague, Bredius 77; Cassel State Art Collections, Bredius 78). This same old man was depicted by Rembrandt's pupil Gerard Dou in the companion portrait to that of Rembrandt's mother (Cassel), which served as the basis for the identification of the model as Harmen Gerritsz van Rijn, the painter's father. This identification, however, found few partisans because, first, two portraits in this series are dated 1631 (Birmingham Museum and Picture Gallery, Bredius 82) and 1632 (Metropolitan Museum of Art, New York, Bredius 169), while we know that Rembrandt's father died in April 1630; and, second, because a drawing was found bearing the legend *Harman. Gerrits. van de Rijn* that portrayed a completely different man (Ashmolean Museum, Oxford, Benesch 56 R). The old man in question is to be connected only with Rembrandt's Leyden period, which might seem to justify his identification as the painter's father. But L. Münz, who made a special study of portraits of Rembrandt's parents, comes to the only possible conclusion — at least from our point of view: "At the present date there is no painting that can justly be considered as an authentic portrait of Rembrandt's father."
Analogies permit us to date the Hermitage painting about 1629—30. The picture is in good condition. Old overpainting is apparent all over the vertical seam in the upper right-hand part of the panel, as well as on the beret, breastplate and background.

PROVENANCE:

Until 1740	Collection of Pierre Crozat, Paris
Until 1750	Collection of François Crozat, Baron du Châtel, Paris
Until 1772	Collection of Crozat, Baron de Thiers, Paris
1772	Acquired for the Hermitage

EXHIBITIONS:

1936	Rembrandt. Moscow — Leningrad (Cat., p. 43, No 2)
1956	Rembrandt and His School. Moscow — Leningrad (Cat., p. 49)
1969—70	Rembrandt, His Precursors and Followers. Leningrad (Cat., p. 18, No 1)

LITERATURE:

Имп. Эрмитаж 1863—1916, № 814; Bode 1873, S. 8; Bode 1883, S. 379; A. M. Hind, "The Portraits of Rembrandt's Father", *The Burlington Magazine*, VIII, 1905—6, p. 426; Valentiner 1909, S. 39; Hofstede de Groot 1915, Nr 681; Bauch 1933, S. 136—137, 197—198; Benesch 1935, S. 4; Rosenberg 1948, p. 9; L. Münz, «Rembrandts Bild von Mutter und Vater», *Jahrbuch der kunsthistorischen Sammlungen in Wien*, N. F., XIV, 1953, S. 141; Левинсон-Лессинг 1956, с. V; Гос. Эрмитаж 1958, с. 251; Levinson-Lessing 1964, No 69; Фехнер 1965, № 2; Bauch 1966, Nr 117; Gerson 1968, No 49; Bredius, No 80.

Rubens. Portrait of Caspar Gevartius.
Ca. 1628.
Fine Arts Museum, Antwerp

3. PORTRAIT OF A SCHOLAR

Oil on canvas, relined. 104 × 92 cm
Signed with a monogram and dated in the upper right-hand corner: *RHL 1631*
The Hermitage, Leningrad. No 741

In the early autumn of 1631 Rembrandt moved from Leyden to Amsterdam. Arnold Houbraken, the painter's first biographer, gives us the exact reasons for this decision: "And since he often had to go to Amsterdam to paint portraits and other works, and seeing that the conditions in that city were favourable and good for his advancement, he found it wise to make his home there" (see A. Houbraken, *De groote Schouburgh...*, Amsterdam, 1718).
Some of the portraits which Rembrandt painted in Amsterdam in 1631, are preserved to the present time: these are the portrait of the Amsterdam merchant Nicolaes Ruts (Frick Collection, New York), and the Hermitage *Portrait of a Scholar*.
There was a time when, on G. Waagen's suggestion, the Hermitage portrait was thought to depict the famous Amsterdam writing master Lieven Coppenol. Later, when the real Coppenol portrait was discovered and Waagen's suggestion discarded, the opinions of specialists were divided. According to W. Bode, this was the portrait of a Leyden University professor, E. Michel saw in it a merchant checking his books, while R. Hamann and A. Bredius believed it to be the portrait of an Amsterdam or Leyden scholar. The writing one can discern on the folio pages makes E. Michel's assumption doubtful: this is no accountant's book. But it is possible that the man portrayed was a statesman, or perhaps somebody belonging to the municipal authorities.
In his early commissioned portraits, Rembrandt followed the Flemish standards of that period. The standard in this case was the *Portrait of Caspar Gevartius* painted by Rubens about 1628 (Fine Arts Museum, Antwerp). But Rembrandt interprets the Flemish prototype in his own way, almost eliminating the element of posing stressed by Rubens. Thus the portrait becomes less pompous and official: it is simpler and more intimate than Rubens's. The painter's preoccupation with real life makes him convey the model's hunched posture, as well as the exact position of his hands while writing. We even discern a slight dissatisfaction in the scholar's glance, psychologically justified in the case of someone disturbed while working. The painting's subdued colour scheme — the black and white tones of the dress (the severe Spanish costume was not yet out of fashion) and the greenish-grey background, the calm outlines of the light and dark areas, and the unusual, almost square shape of the canvas, give the portrait a serious, significant and balanced aspect — qualities held in especially high esteem in Dutch society of the early seventeeth century.
The manner of painting is also serene, solid and unperturbed. The strokes strictly follow the form, featuring its peculiarities, the volume, and the character of the surface. Thanks to this, the observer not only sees but almost feels the soft, though yellowing and flabby skin of the scholar's hands, the cold surface of the folio page, the friable material of the tablecloth. The painter plays off their diametrically opposed qualities through both colour and texture.
Portrait of a Scholar enjoyed, in all evidence, a great success. Soon Rembrandt received a commission for his most important portrait of that period — *The Anatomy Lesson of Doctor Tulp* (Mauritshuis Royal Picture Gallery, The Hague), which he painted in the same style as his *Portrait of a Scholar* and *Portrait of Nicolaes Ruts*. The picture is in good condition. Slight overpainting of the damaged layer, applied during restoration, is apparent on the dress below and along the entire right-hand border of the canvas.

PROVENANCE:

Until 1769   Count Brühl Collection, Dresden
        1769   Acquired for the Hermitage

EXHIBITIONS:

1936   Rembrandt. Moscow — Leningrad (Cat., p. 43, No 3)
1956   Rembrandt and His School. Moscow — Leningrad (Cat., pp. 49—50)
1968   Masterpieces of Rembrandt. Tokyo — Kioto (Cat. No 1)
1968—69   Old Masters from the Hermitage. Belgrade (Cat. No 35)
1969—70   Rembrandt, His Precursors and Followers. Leningrad (Cat., p. 18, No 2)
1976   Master Paintings from the Hermitage and State Russian Museum, Leningrad. Win-
            nipeg (Cat. No 18)

LITERATURE:

Имп. Эрмитаж 1863—1916, № 808; Bode 1883, S. 382; Valentiner 1909, S. 65; Hofstede de
Groot 1915, Nr 775; Weisbach 1926, S. 265; Benesch 1935, S. 11; Hamann 1948, S. 138; Левинсон-Лессинг 1956, с. VI; Knuttel 1956, blz. 45; Гос. Эрмитаж 1958, с. 251; Фехнер 1965,
№ 3; Bauch 1966, Nr 349; Gerson 1968, No 54; Bredius, No 146.

Rembrandt's School. The Adoration of the Magi.
Art Gallery, Gothenburg

The Adoration of the Magi.
Drawing. 1630s.
National Library, Turin

4. THE ADORATION OF THE MAGI

Oil on paper pasted on canvas, relined. 45 × 39 cm. Grisaille
Signed and dated below centre, right: *Rembrandt f. 1632*
The Hermitage, Leningrad. No 7765

In the 1630s Rembrandt produced several grisailles, the last of which is dated 1641. Together with the Hermitage painting, we know of seven. Rembrandt's grisailles are usually bitonal: brown (sepia) and grey or light blue. Such, too, is *The Adoration of the Magi* of the Hermitage collection, where the foreground is pure sepia, while the background is done in cold grey tones that seem almost bluish thanks to the masterly and exact correlation with the warmer foreground. The overall effect is one of rare beauty.

This painting was only recently recognized as a Rembrandt original. Its composition is nearly identical to that of the picture on the same subject in the Gothenburg Art Gallery, published as a Rembrandt original eight years before the acquisition of the Hermitage painting. There is nothing strange, therefore, in the fact that Hermitage curators paid little attention to this new grisaille and immediately qualified it as a "copy of Rembrandt's original in Sweden". Even the fact that the Hermitage picture seemed to be authentically signed and dated was ignored, though the Swedish work had no signature whatsoever. *The Adoration of the Magi* was put in the Hermitage store-rooms. It was not included in any catalogues, never published and, with the exception of museum workers, remained absolutely unknown.

Later on, however, the masterly quality of the painting, as well as the signature and date, drew attention and provoked a comparison with the Gothenburg picture. This comparison brought about the surprising conclusion that the Hermitage painting was far superior. What is more, the Hermitage *Adoration of the Magi*, both in its iconographic features and manner of execution, bears all the particularities of Rembrandt's style of the 1630s.

X-ray investigation furnished exceedingly valuable information. It showed serious alterations introduced by the author in the process of work — such alterations may serve as irrefutable proof of the painting being the original result of the artist's creative search, not a copy. It was discovered, for instance, that the figure of the King in the first version was placed somewhat more to the right and further in the background; one can clearly discern the original position of the large parasol. The older King's cloak was brightly lit along its border, much in the manner of Rembrandt's *Simon in the Temple* (Mauritshuis Royal Picture Gallery, The Hague) or his *St Peter in Prison* (1631, Merode-Westerloo Collection, Brussels). It was also shown that, in the first version, the figure of the kneeling youth who holds a cup in his hand was totally absent (Rembrandt had seen similar figures of kneeling youths with cups in their hands in Lastman's paintings). Their prototypes may also be found in Italian Renaissance paintings. However, the most likely assumption would be that Rembrandt was inspired here by Rubens's works, well known thanks to engravings. In general, it must be said that *The Adoration of the Magi* was not produced by Rembrandt without Rubens in mind: the Flemish master's influence is apparent here both in the general compositional structure and in several other aspects of the painting.

To include the kneeling youth into the composition, Rembrandt had to slightly alter the figure of the man who stands behind the youth on the stairs: as the X-rays show, Rembrandt hid his legs by a dais. Simultaneously, he applied the now necessary shadow to the kneeling king's back. Evidently in the first version there was also a second source of light (in the right-hand background), such as is found in other Rembrandt paintings of that period. All this brings us

The Adoration of the Magi.
Drawing. *Ca.* 1632.
Print Room, Dahlem Museum, Berlin

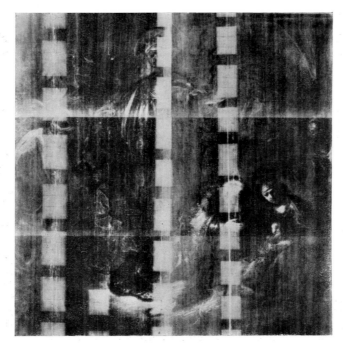

Rembrandt's School. The Adoration of the Magi
(X-ray photograph). Art Gallery, Gothenburg

to the conclusion that, far from the Hermitage painting being a copy of the Gothenburg work, the situation is exactly the opposite: ours is the original, while the Swedish painting is a copy. Two of Rembrandt's drawings on the same subject may be linked to the Hermitage painting. One, in the Dahlem Museum Print Room, Berlin (Benesch 160), shows the Holy Family and the old magus in a fashion similar to the Hermitage painting, but turned in the opposite direction. Jakob Rosenberg dates this drawing 1632, while Benesch sees here a return to the manner of 1632, typical of Rembrandt's art of the 1637—39 period. The other drawing is the property of the Turin National Library. It resembles the Hermitage painting in what concerns the Holy Family group and the old magus, both placed to the right and turned as in the canvas, and also the group of soldiers descending the stairs. Opinions as to the Turin drawing's date differ even more than in the case of that of the Dahlem Museum Print Room. Scholars suggest different dates between 1634 and 1642. The reason for these contradictions may be found in the fact that in this drawing, painted after the Hermitage picture, Rembrandt uses and repeats elements discovered in 1632.

The painting's condition may be esteemed as rather good, though the underlying coat is friable. Only in the right part of the picture there is overpainting of the paint losses, applied during restoration along three vertical foldings.

This painting may have been the one mentioned in the inventory of the Prince of Orange collection, drawn *ca.* 1714, which lists "a small Rembrandt painting, *The Adoration of the Magi*". No other Rembrandt painting known today could have fitted that description.

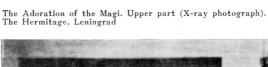

The Adoration of the Magi. Upper part (X-ray photograph).
The Hermitage, Leningrad

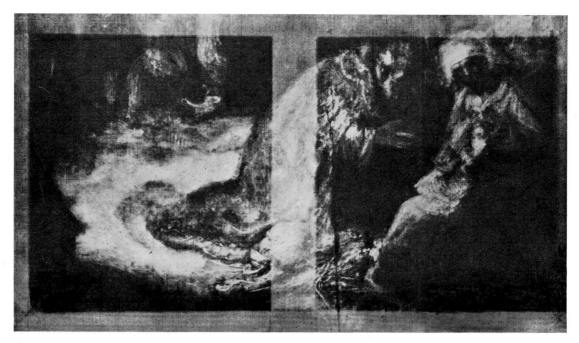

The Adoration of the Magi. Lower part (X-ray photograph).
The Hermitage, Leningrad

PROVENANCE:

Until 1923   Paskevich Collection, Petrograd
    1923   The Hermitage

EXHIBITIONS:

1968—69   The Age of Rembrandt. Tokyo — Kioto (Cat. No 44)
1969—70   Rembrandt, His Precursors and Followers. Leningrad (Cat., pp. 18—19, No 3)
   1976   Seventeenth Century Dutch Painting in the Hermitage. Tallinn (Cat., p. 5)

LITERATURE:

И. Линник, «Вновь открытая картина Рембрандта в Эрмитаже», *Сообщения Государственного Эрмитажа*, XXIX, 1968, с. 26—28; I. Linnik, «*Die Anbetung der Könige* von Rembrandt», *Pantheon*, XXVII, Januar — Februar 1969, S. 36—41; Bredius, p. 604, No 541; *Rembrandt 1669/1969. Tentoonstelling ter herdenking van Rembrandts sterfdag op 4 oktober 1669*, Rijksmuseum, Amsterdam [Catalogus], blz. 121; Yu. Kuznetsov, "Rembrandt Discoveries at the Hermitage", *Apollo*, December 1974, pp. 488—490.

5. PORTRAIT OF A BOY

Oil on oak, cradled. 67 × 47.5 cm. Top and bottom rounded.
The Hermitage, Leningrad. No 724

In Rembrandt's works of the 1633—34 period, we often come across a round-faced boy with large brown eyes, wearing earrings and dressed in fantastic apparel. The boy's likeness to Saskia van Uylenburgh and certain details of Rembrandt's biography, who during those years lived in the house of Saskia's uncle, the art dealer Hendrick van Uylenburgh, support H. Wijnman's identification of the model as Hendrick's eight-year-old son Gerrit. A certain similarity, more iconographic than stylistic, between the Hermitage painting and the 1633 miniature portraits of the same boy (one of unknown origin, Bredius 187; another in the Wallace Collection, London, Bredius 188), allows us to refer *Portrait of a Boy* to the same year, 1633.
Rembrandt's authorship of this entire group, including the portraits in the Rothschild Collection, Ferrières, and in the Duke of Portland Collection, Welbeck Abbey, is questionable. The first doubts about the Hermitage portrait were voiced by G. Waagen: upon his advice the work was included in the 1863 Hermitage catalogue as belonging to Govaert Flinck. Another portrait, also ascribed to Flinck, but with more certainty, is in a private Dutch collection, although J. von Moltke, the author of a monograph on Govaert Flinck, has not included it in his catalogue of this painter's works. W. Martin, who also questioned Rembrandt's authorship, suggested that this group of portraits, with one exception, was repainted by I. Jouderville. This latter assumption is as difficult to prove as it is to refute: as yet we know too little about this Rembrandt's pupil. In what concerns Flinck, these portraits indeed bear a certain resemblance to his work both in the colour scheme, based on a combination of cold wine-red shades with ochre and greenish browns, and in the somewhat sentimental treatment of the subject. We know, however, that this particular colour scheme was almost entirely borrowed by the pupil from his teacher. As for the element of sentimentality, it is easily explained, in this case, by the subject-matter — like Flinck, Rembrandt could have been influenced by the charm of a tender child's face. We know that the same model appears as a cherub in the 1634 painting *Vanitas* (Baron Bentinck Collection, Paris, Bredius 470), which is probably a joint work of Rembrandt and Flinck. When making a final judgement as to the author of the Hermitage canvas, one must also keep in mind that Flinck attained the sufficient degree of workmanship only around 1637, when he painted the Hermitage *Portrait of a Young Man* (No 782), probably depicting Rembrandt. At this time the model, if painted by Flinck from nature, should have looked much older. The picture's condition is good. Slight overpainting is apparent only along the seam in the left part of the canvas.

PROVENANCE:
Between 1783 and 1797 Acquired for the Hermitage

EXHIBITIONS:
1956   Rembrandt and His School. Moscow — Leningrad (Cat., p. 50)
1969—70   Rembrandt, His Precursors and Followers. Leningrad (Cat., p. 19, No 4)

LITERATURE:
Имп. Эрмитаж 1863—1916, № 843; Valentiner 1909, S. 40; Hofstede de Groot 1915, Nr 492; W. Martin, *Der Kunstwanderer*, 3, 1921/22, S. 30; Hamann 1948, S. 46; H. F. Wijnman, «Rembrandt en Hendrick Uylenburgh te Amsterdam», *Maanblad Amstelodamum*, 43, 1956, blz. 202; Левинсон-Лессинг 1956, с. VIII; Гос. Эрмитаж 1958, с. 251; Фехнер 1965, № 5; Bauch 1966, Nr. 151; Gerson 1968, No 131; Bredius, No 186.

Portrait of a Young Woman with
Flowers in Her Hair. 1634. National
Gallery of Scotland, Edinburgh

6. PORTRAIT OF A YOUNG MAN WITH A LACE COLLAR

Oil on oak, cradled. 70 × 52 cm. Oval
Signed and dated right, near the shoulder: *Rembrandt f. 1634*
The Hermitage, Leningrad. No 725

In the mid-1630s Rembrandt was very much in vogue as a portrait painter; commissions poured down on him, a wealth of portraits resulting: official full-lengths, less ostentatious half-lengths and busts. *Portrait of a Young Man with a Lace Collar* and its companion *Portrait of a Young Woman with Flowers in Her Hair* (National Gallery of Scotland, Edinburgh, Bredius 345) both belonged to the modest type of portrait, not beyond the means of most customers. Judging from the man's and woman's age, the portraits were a wedding commission. The severe pose and ceremonial dress proper to the solemn occasion are somewhat counterbalanced by the oval form of the portraits, while the rather stereotype smile is lighted by the shining eyes.
The oval form was Rembrandt's favourite in companion portraits of that period. Some forty portraits of this type, dated between 1632 and 1635, have reached us, not counting a dozen that bear no date but evidently belong to the same period.
In what concerns the brushwork of *Portrait of a Young Man with a Lace Collar*, it is somewhat inferior to its pendant. The explanation, strangely enough, lies in the technique and laws of the genre itself. One of the peculiarities of companion portraits is their prescribed correlation; to begin with, the faces must be turned toward each other. Hence, the man, always on the left, is slightly turned to the right, while the woman, on the right, must look left. But since both models are usually lighted from a source to their left, just as the canvas itself (otherwise the painter's right hand holding the brush would block the light), the man is always in a less enviable position: a deep shade covers a large part of his face. And since Rembrandt applied impasto only to lighted areas, whereas the shaded ones were only slightly touched, the underpainting, and at times even the structure of the canvas or panel, visible in the shaded areas, lend the man's portrait a less "complete" quality. We believe this explains H. Gerson's comment that the Hermitage portrait is "slightly weaker in quality" than its pendant of the Edinburgh Gallery. The picture is in good condition. Old overpainting is apparent on the dress at the bottom.

PROVENANCE:

Until 1829   Collection of the Duchess of Saint-Leu, Paris
      1829   Acquired for the Hermitage

EXHIBITIONS:

1936   Rembrandt. Moscow—Leningrad (Cat., p. 43, No 4)
1956   Rembrandt and His School. Moscow—Leningrad (Cat., p. 51)
1969—70   Rembrandt, His Precursors and Followers. Leningrad (Cat., p. 19, No 5)

LITERATURE:

Имп. Эрмитаж 1863—1916, № 828; Bode 1873, S. 8; Valentiner 1909, S. 200; Hofstede de Groot 1915, Nr 777; Benesch 1935, S. 17; Левинсон-Лессинг 1956, с. VI—VII; Гос. Эрмитаж 1958, с. 252; Фехнер 1965, № 4; Gerson 1968, No 166; Bredius, No 196.

Saskia as Flora.
1635. National Gallery, London

Saskia. 1633. Drawing.
Print Room, Dahlem Museum,
Berlin

7. SASKIA AS FLORA

Oil on canvas, relined. 125 × 101 cm
Signed and dated at bottom, left: *Rembrandt. f. 1634*
The Hermitage, Leningrad. No 732

The painter here depicted his first wife Saskia van Uylenburgh, daughter of the Burgomaster of Leeuwarden Rumbartus van Uylenburgh, as Flora, the Roman goddess of flowers and spring. In 1633 Rembrandt and Saskia were engaged, and a year later married. Both of these events were reflected in his paintings. Three days after their engagement, Rembrandt made a drawing in silver point where Saskia is depicted in a broad-brimmed hat, decorated with flowers, and holding a flower in one hand (Dahlem Museum Print Room, Berlin). The drawing bears a touching inscription: "Here is depicted my wife, aged 21, on the third day of our engagement, June 8, 1633." *Portrait of Saskia* (Art Gallery of the Old Masters, Dresden) is dated the same year. In 1634 the painter produced *Flora*. One year later, preserving the general idea, but changing the model's posture, Rembrandt painted a new version of Saskia as Flora (National Gallery, London).

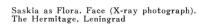
Saskia as Flora. Face (X-ray photograph).
The Hermitage, Leningrad

It is commonly accepted that during those years the model's inner world was of no special interest to the painter. He takes pleasure in depicting the details of the model's apparel and accessories. The precious fabric that falls in heavy folds and the bright flowers that crown the model's head and entwine the staff are painted no less lovingly than the face. But a comparison of the London and Hermitage *Floras* is enough to see how delicately the artist conveys his model's inner being. The Hermitage *Flora* is a youthful Saskia, almost a child, embarrassed by the finery of her dress: the heavy garland has forced her to slightly incline her head and lower her eyes, she grasps the staff with hesitating and uncertain hands and holds back the heavy folds of her cape. In the National Gallery painting, Saskia is but a year older, but there we see a young woman well aware of her power, who plays the role of a goddess with ease, her head proudly lifted and shoulders thrown back.

The manner of *Flora* still shows the influence of Rembrandt's teacher, Pieter Lastman. This is especially evident if one compares the brush lines of the apparel and drapings. However, the variegation of technique and devices, as witnessed by the delicate touch of the face and hands and the thick strokes conveying the relief of the fabric, bespeaks the painter's intense search for an artistic idiom of his own. In old inventories and catalogues of the Hermitage, *Flora* is called *The Jewish Bride* or *The Young Jewess*. These titles find their source in Rembrandt's etching of 1635 called *The Great Jewish Bride* (Bartsch 340), to which both the Hermitage and London paintings bear a definite resemblance, especially in what concerns the face, coiffure and apparel. But the etching's title, universally accepted from the early eighteenth century, is purely conventional. Its subject is, by all probabilities, *Esther Making Ready to Meet Ahasuerus*; its model was also Saskia, as testified to by the drawing of the Stockholm National Museum (Benesch 292).

Delving into the history of the Hermitage painting, one also encounters the title *Portrait of a Lady as a Shepherdess on a Landscape Background, Depicted Full-life*. It was under this title that the painting figured at the sale of the Harmen Arents collection in Amsterdam in 1770. This title was no accident. In the first half of the seventeenth century, portraits in the guise of shepherds or shepherdesses were very common in Holland. The impulse here was given by P. Hooft's pastoral *Granida and Daifilo* (ca. 1605). In 1636, Rembrandt's pupil Govaert Flinck, following the general fashion, produced two companion portraits, in which his teacher was depicted as Daifilo (Rijksmuseum, Amsterdam), and his wife Saskia as Granida (Herzog Anton Ulrich Museum, Brunswick). The pastoral motif, Saskia as a young bride in a straw hat decorated with flowers, probably suggested the basic concept of *Flora*. There is another drawing that both chronologically and formally may be placed somewhere between the Berlin drawing and the Hermitage and London *Floras*. This is *Young Woman in a Broad-brimmed Hat and Holding a Staff* (Amsterdam Print Room). Seymour Slive sees in this drawing a study of Flora's figure. Admitting the formal link between this drawing and the two *Floras*, we are inclined to believe the young woman in the Hermitage portrait to be a shepherdess, not Flora, since on her right hip she carries a gourd. But in that case, a new stage is evident in the painter's conceptual evolution: that in which Saskia does indeed exist as a shepherdess. Some scholars continue to believe that both paintings depict Rembrandt's wife as an Arcadian shepherdess (E. Kieser, N. MacLaren).

There is, however, a possibility that, while painting the Hermitage canvas, the artist discarded his original design and chose to depict his wife as Flora. The decisive factor here probably was his seeing Titian's *Flora* (Uffizi, Florence), which was then part of Alfonso Lopez's Amsterdam collection. Titian's canvas made a great impression on Rembrandt. He kept it in mind when painting *Saskia with a Flower* (Art Gallery of the Old Masters, Dresden) in 1641, and also in 1656, when Hendrickje Stoffels posed for a new *Flora* (Metropolitan Museum of Art, New York). Finally, seventeenth century sources furnish the genuine title of the painting. This is Rembrandt's own inscription of 1635 on the reverse of a drawing in the Dahlem Museum Print Room, Berlin (Benesch 448). Here he mentions the sales of paintings done by his pupils: the subject is Flora. These paintings, as scholars correctly assume, were copies of the Hermitage or the London canvases. Thus, the conclusion reached first by E. Michel in 1893, that the artist depicted Saskia as Flora, found its documental confirmation.

As a typical work of the first half of the 1630s, based on a mythological subject, *Flora* has many analogies in other Rembrandt paintings, inspired by Saskia: *Bellona* (1633, Metropolitan Museum of Art, New York), *Minerva* (1635, J. Weitzner Collection, London) and *Sophonisba* (1634, Prado, Madrid). The Hermitage painting conveys the same idea of antiquity and shows the same style and iconographic traits as were Rembrandt's during those years.

The painting is in good condition. Slight overpainting is discernible on Flora's right eyelid and on the background, where it is applied over the losses of paint and priming.

PROVENANCE:

1770   On sale at the Harmen Arents auction, Amsterdam (sale cancelled since no one offered more than the lot's price of 2,600 florins)

EXHIBITIONS:

1936	Rembrandt. Moscow—Leningrad (Cat., p. 43, No 5)
1956	Rembrandt. Amsterdam—Rotterdam (Cat., p. 51, No 24)
1968	Masterpieces of Rembrandt. Tokyo—Kioto (Cat. No 3)
1969—70	Rembrandt, His Precursors and Followers. Leningrad (Cat., pp. 19—20, No 6)
1972	Masterpieces from the Hermitage, Leningrad, and the Pushkin Museum of Fine Arts, Moscow. Dresden (Cat. No 41)
1974	Flemish and Dutch Masters in the Hermitage, Leningrad. Havre (Cat. No 17)
1975—76	Master Paintings from the Hermitage and the State Russian Museum, Leningrad. Washington, D.C.; New York, N.Y.; Detroit, Michigan; Los Angeles, California; Houston, Texas (Cat. No 18)
1976	Master Paintings from the Hermitage and the Russian Museum, Leningrad. Mexico (Cat. No 18)

LITERATURE:

Имп. Эрмитаж 1863—1916, № 812; Bode 1883, S. 424; H. Voss, «Rembrandt und Tizian», *Repertorium für Kunstwissenschaft*, 28, 1905, S. 158; Valentiner 1909, S. 137; Hofstede de Groot 1915, Nr 206; W. Drost, *Barockmalerei in den germanischen Ländern*, Wildpark—Potsdam, 1926, S. 153; Weisbach 1926, S. 235; Benesch 1935, S. 17; E. Kieser, «Über Rembrandts Verhältnis zur Antike», *Zeitschrift für Kunstgeschichte*, 10, 1941/42, S. 155; Hamann 1948, S. 215—216; Rosenberg 1948, p. 43; Левинсон-Лессинг 1956, c. VIII; Knuttel 1956, blz. 85; Гос. Эрмитаж 1958, c. 251; J. Held, "Flora Goddess and Courtesan", *De artibus opuscula: Essays in Honor of Erwin Panofsky*, New York, 1961, pp. 201—218; Levinson-Lessing 1964, Nos 70, 71; Фехнер 1965, № 6; Gerson 1968, No 92; Haak 1968, blz. 104; Bredius, No 102; M. Louttit, "The Romantic Dress of Saskia van Uylenborch", *The Burlington Magazine*, May 1973, pp. 318, 322.

The Incredulity of St Thomas. 1650. Etching

8. THE INCREDULITY OF ST THOMAS

Oil on oak. 50 × 51 cm
Signed and dated in the lower left-hand corner: *Rembrandt f. 1634*
The Pushkin Museum of Fine Arts, Moscow. No 2619

According to the Gospel, the apostle Thomas refused to believe in the resurrection of Christ, saying, "Except I shall see in his hands the print of the nails, and put my finger into the print of the nails, and thrust my hand into his side, I will not believe." Then Christ, appearing in the midst of his disciples, told Thomas to behold his hands, and to reach his hand and thrust it into his side, and said, "Because thou hast seen me, thou hast believed: blessed are they that have not seen, and yet have believed" (*John*, 20. 25, 29).
This subject often attracted the attention of seventeenth century painters. Rembrandt's picture can be regarded as one of its most detailed and exhaustive illustrations. The painter strives to portray the evangelic episode in the most striking fashion, and builds the composition corre-

The Incredulity of St Thomas (infra-red photograph).
The Pushkin Museum of Fine Arts, Moscow

The Incredulity of St Thomas. Detail (ultraviolet photograph).
The Pushkin Museum of Fine Arts, Moscow

spondingly. The figures, placed at different levels, some standing, some sitting, others kneeling, mingle in such a way as to set off Christ and St Thomas, simultaneously conveying the emotions of all the spectators. Standing in a half-circle, they contrast with Thomas who reels back in horror. The young painter somewhat naively depicts anxiety, surprise, interest and the urge to see everything with one's own eyes as the appropriate and normal feelings of those who are witnessing a miracle; of all the protagonists, probably the most convincing is the man in the right-hand corner who, bent in prayer, does not dare lift his eyes; he confirms, as it were, Christ's words concerning those who have not seen but have believed. Finally, the man asleep in the foreground serves as a symbol of ignorance and mental blindness. The deplorable light-mindedness of people who ignore great revelations was one of the main themes of Dutch art in the sixteenth century. In the seventeenth it became secondary and was less often found. Rembrandt's portrayal of the sleeping man seems perfectly natural, the didactic meaning is not obvious, although the painter certainly had it in mind.

The picture is carefully finished only in its central, lighted part. In other areas the painter applies a more or less rough hand. His characteristic techniques are most apparent in the portrayal of the sleeping man (St John?) and the objects lying next to him. The dark red cloak

The Incredulity of St Thomas. Detail (X-ray photograph).
The Pushkin Museum of Fine Arts, Moscow

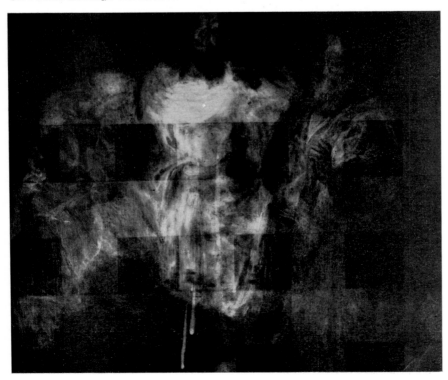

under his head is painted with brusque jelly-like dabs; the cloak and the prop underneath it are outlined with bold strokes of black. These lines, which give the objects a definite form, are strikingly evident in infra-red photography. They remind one of the bold manner of Rembrandt the draughtsman. The painting here is rather incomplete, while in the central part the artist brilliantly depicts the embroidery of St Thomas's light blue dress. The tinted priming, discernible in many places as a thin coating of reddish brown, gives the coloration a warm glow. The variegated, bold and beautiful painting is proof of a high degree of mastery. X-ray investigation shows that the original design underwent several changes in the process of painting. In the underpainting, a bright area spreads to the left of the man in black who kneels in the foreground, his back turned to the viewer. Later the artist partially covered this bright spot with dark glaze, including this figure in the group to Christ's left. The figures of Christ and St Thomas also underwent considerable changes.

The picture is in good condition. The overpainting done during restoration is applied mainly to the background and to the black dress of the kneeling man in the foreground.

The theme of incredulity and belief of the evangelic tale, as well as the theme of belief *per se* versus belief on proof, was certainly not exhausted in Rembrandt's picture of 1634. It was given a fundamentally different interpretation later, in his etching of 1650 (Bartsch 89). Here the disciples stand apart in awe, Christ is left alone. Thomas has fallen on his knees and fears to lift his eyes to the blinding revelation. In essence this etching contradicts the earlier painting's interpretation of the Gospel. However, as in many other works of the 1630s, the painting shows evidence of the seed that will grow and develop, forming Rembrandt's creative credo.

PROVENANCE:

1733	F. van Dijck Collection, The Hague
1755	Lennep Collection, Amsterdam
1759	Gotzkowsky Collection, Berlin
1764	Acquired for the Hermitage
1930	The Pushkin Museum of Fine Arts, Moscow

EXHIBITIONS:

1936	Rembrandt. Moscow—Leningrad (Cat., p. 44, No 7)
1956	Rembrandt and His School. Moscow—Leningrad (Cat., pp. 50—51)
1968	Masterpieces of Rembrandt. Tokyo—Kioto (Cat. No 4)
1969	Rembrandt. Moscow (Cat., pp. 13, 17)

LITERATURE:

Terwesten 1770, blz. 42, Nr 79; Catalogue 1774, N° 602; Notice 1828, p. 79, 136; Livret 1838, p. 224, N° 95 (as Rembrandt's school); Имп. Эрмитаж 1863—1916, № 801; Waagen 1864, S. 176; Bode 1873, S. 11; Bode 1883, S. 436; Bode — Hofstede de Groot 1897—1905, Nr 133; Valentiner 1909, S. 159; Hofstede de Groot 1915, S. 92, Nr 148; Weisbach 1926, S. 140—141; Benesch 1935, S. 17; Левинсон-Лессинг 1956, с. VIII; Каталог ГМИИ 1961, с. 155; Фехнер 1965, № 7, с. 52—55; Bauch 1966, Nr 60; Gerson 1968, p. 37, 220, 491, No 67; Bredius, No 552; Исследование картин Рембрандта, с. 395—400.

Vorstermann. The Descent from
the Cross. 1620. Engraving

The Descent from the Cross.
1633. Etching

9. THE DESCENT FROM THE CROSS

Oil on canvas, relined. 158 × 117 cm
Signed and dated at bottom, centre: *Rembrandt f. 1634*
The Hermitage, Leningrad. No 753

The painting is an illustration of the evangelic legend concerning Joseph of Arimathaea, Nico-demus and other disciples of Christ who, having been granted permission by Pilate, took the dead Christ's body from the cross, wound it in linen clothes and buried it (*Matthew*, 27. 57—59; *Mark*, 15. 45—46; *Luke*, 23. 52—53; *John*, 19. 40).
The Gospel story is rendered here by Rembrandt with breath-taking power. The tragic death of the teacher and son steeps the participants of the nocturnal scene in sorrow. The painter studies their faces, striving to read their personal response to the event. His portrayal of the swooning Mary, of the weeping and wailing women, of the suffering and grief-stricken men, of the children's mixture of fear and curiosity is masterful.
Writing to the Stadholder's secretary Constantyn Huygens, the painter defined his artistic pur-pose as striving to convey "the greatest and the most natural movement" ("die meeste ende die naetuereelste beweechgelickheyt"), meaning not so much outward dynamics as movements of the spirit. Contemporaries must also have appreciated these new qualities of his art. At any rate, the Dutch poet Jan Baptist Wellekens (1658—1726) interpreted the painting, then in the collection of Valerius de Roever, exactly as Rembrandt had intended it to be interpreted: "There we see your / Crucifixion, so marvellously pictured: / The griefstricken mother has faint-ed, / Each plays his sad part."
Roever himself highly valued the painting. Entering it under No 1 of his inventory, he wrote: "A very significant and artistic work of Rembrandt van Rijn, the best of all his known paintings."
The Descent from the Cross of the Hermitage collection is the second of two versions. A year prior to that, in 1633, Rembrandt painted the first version (Alte Pinakothek, Munich, Bredius 550), which became part of a series of three pictures. The others were *The Crucifixion*, dated 1631, now in the Church of Le Mas D'Agenais in France (Bartsch 543 A), and *Elevation of the Cross* produced between 1631 and 1633, now in the Alte Pinakothek, Munich (Bartsch 548). The first version of *Descent from the Cross*, together with *Elevation of the Cross*, was acquired by the Stadholder of the Netherlands Frederick Henry of Nassau, Prince of Orange, probably on the advice of Constantyn Huygens. This was followed by a commission for three more paintings of the Passion, work on which continued for many years. Rembrandt finished *The Ascension* (Bredius 557) in January—February of 1636, and *The Entombment* (Bredius 560) and *Resurrection* (Bredius 561) three years later, in 1639. Strangely enough, this triad, commis-sioned by the Prince and to which Rembrandt "applied much diligence", as he himself admits, is far inferior to the Hermitage *Descent from the Cross*, painted during the same period as a kind of extra-curricular activity; it remained in the painter's own collection until 1656.
For this series, as well as for the Hermitage painting on the same Passion subject, Rembrandt used the famous canvas of Rubens as a spring-board, turning to certain compositional motifs of the great Flemish painter and striving to surpass him in the depiction of the protagonists' inner state. The composition of the Munich version of *The Descent from the Cross* was based on the celebrated Rubens altarpiece in Antwerp, known to Rembrandt thanks to the engrav-ing by Lucas Vorsterman. In Rembrandt's painting the position of Christ's body, as well as that of certain other figures, reminds one of Rubens, yet this similarity serves only to reveal the diametrically opposed principles of the two great painters. If neither grief nor even death

can disfigure the ideal beauty of Rubens's hero, Rembrandt sticks to severe realism: in his tragedy people's faces are distorted by grief and suffering, and yet they remain beautiful in their emotions.

In that same year of 1633 Rembrandt makes an engraving of his painting, with certain changes in the etching (Bartsch 81). The composition of the etching was later repeated in the Hermitage picture. Rembrandt makes the scene nocturnal, so that the light, somewhat obscure in the first version and openly mystic in the etching (a ray from heaven!), now comes from a definite source; namely, from three candles, or torches, that, as it were, dramatically bring to the fore the three central points of the narrative. The use of light organizing a multifigure scene into an entity, while at the same time accentuating the individual emotions of each person, was yet another of Rembrandt's achievements in this painting.

A free-style copy of Rembrandt's original was made in his studio in the early 1650s; it is now to be seen in the National Gallery of Art in Washington (Bredius 584).

High impasto is applied to the central part of the painting characterized by a concentration of the brightest spots of light. Here a weak cohesion of the priming and paint with the underlying coat presents a constant threat of losses. The child's left hand and the cape hiding the torch from the spectators are repainted. Considerable losses are apparent in the lower left-hand corner of the painting.

PROVENANCE:

Until 1656	The artist's collection, Amsterdam
Until 1693	Collection of Valerius de Roever Sr., Amsterdam
Until 1703	Collection of Catherine Elizabeth Bode, widow of Valerius de Roever Sr., Amsterdam
Until 1739	Collection of Valerius de Roever Jr., Delft
1750	Cassel Picture Gallery
1806	Malmaison Collection of the Empress Josephine
1814	Acquired for the Hermitage

EXHIBITIONS:

1936	Rembrandt. Moscow—Leningrad (Cat., p. 44, No 6)
1956	Rembrandt and His School. Moscow — Leningrad (exhibited only in Leningrad, Cat., pp. 63—64)
1969—70	Rembrandt, His Precursors and Followers. Leningrad (Cat., pp. 20—21, No 7)

LITERATURE:

J. B. Wellekens, *Verscheiden Gedichten*, Amsterdam, 1729, blz. 5, 6; Hoet 1752, II, blz. 396; Имп. Эрмитаж 1863—1916, № 800; Bode 1873, S. 12; Bode 1883, S. 435; Valentiner 1909, S. 164; Hofstede de Groot 1915, Nr 135; Weisbach 1926, S. 133, 137, 465; W. Stechow, «Rembrandts Darstellungen der Kreuzabnahme», *Jahrbuch der preußischen Kunstsammlungen*, 50, 1929, S. 217 ff.; Benesch 1935, S. 13; Rosenberg 1948, pp. 117, 134, 135; Hamann 1948, S. 242; S. Slive, *Rembrandt and His Critics: 1630—1730*, The Hague, 1953, pp. 173—174; Knuttel 1956, blz. 91; Левинсон-Лессинг 1956, с. VIII; Гос. Эрмитаж 1958, с. 252; Фехнер 1965, № 8; Вольская 1966, с. 57—58; Gerson 1968, No 66; Haak 1968, blz. 99; Bredius, No 551.

Abraham's Sacrifice. *Ca.* 1636. Drawing.
British Museum, London

Rembrandt and Govaert Flinck (?).
Abraham's Sacrifice. 1636.
Alte Pinakothek, Munich

10. ABRAHAM'S SACRIFICE

Oil on canvas, transferred from the old one. 193 × 132.5 cm
Signed and dated at bottom, left: *Rembrandt. f. 1635*
The Hermitage, Leningrad. No 727

The mid-1630s were a period when Rembrandt's art was at its closest to the European Baroque style. The outstanding example of this style in Rembrandt's art is the large canvas entitled *Abraham's Sacrifice*. Rembrandt chooses the most dramatic moment of the biblical episode — when Abraham, in obeyance to God's will, is about to plunge his knife into Isaac's neck (*Genesis*, 22. 1—12). At that moment, an angel appears from heaven to stop the offering with which the Lord tempted Abraham. The split second of the happening is emphasized by the falling knife (a device that must have astounded Rembrandt's contemporaries), by the angel hurtling down from above, by the sharp, sudden turn of Abraham's head and by the frightened, surprised expression of his face. The feeling of supreme nervous tension and heightened dramatism is created by the wind-blown folds of the cloak and Abraham's streaming hair, as well as by the flashes of light on the faces and arms, and on Isaac's naked body. The feeling is strengthened by the jagged contours and dynamic splotches of colour, cold blues, yellows and greens. At the same time, the entire composition resembles a beautiful and decorative theatrical performance. The effect of authenticity is destroyed by the Baroque concept, but another, no less important, goal is achieved: the emotional effect of a very high degree.

J. Held, who also mentions the theatrical quality of the composition, reasonably supposes that Rembrandt knew the play by Theodore Beza (1519—1605), *Abraham Sacrifiant*, where the behaviour and emotional state of Abraham, his grief, perplexity and indecision are brought out with uncommon force. Moreover, one of the stage directions explicitly says that Abraham loosens his grip of the dagger, letting it fall to the ground.

A year later, Rembrandt returned to the same subject, as witnessed by one of his drawings (British Museum, London, Benesch 90), a copy of which was made by his pupils in 1636 (Alte Pinakothek, Munich). This version's main compositional innovations are the angel's different position and pose, while iconographic changes include the ram caught in a thicket and afterwards used by Abraham for the offering instead of Isaac.

The Munich painting is largely based on the Pieter Lastman composition, of which there were two versions; one, dated 1661, is in the Louvre, the other was not preserved and is known only thanks to J. van Somer's engraving. The angel approaches Abraham not from the left, as in the Hermitage painting, but from behind, as in the Lastman picture. According to W. Weisbach, the Hermitage version's angel finds its prototype in Titian's *Sacrifice*, painted for the ceiling of the Santa Maria della Salute Chapel in Venice. But both the Hermitage and the Munich canvases preserve the compositional device of Lastman: the gesture of the angel grasping Abraham by the wrist to stay his hand.

The Hermitage painting was transferred to a new canvas in 1850, the priming being white lead. Naturally, X-ray investigations proved futile. There are some minor changes introduced by the author and apparent to the naked eye. The most important is his alteration of the top border of the loincloth which in the first version ran some 3 or 4 cm higher than in the final one. X-ray examination of the Munich painting also proved fruitless, few changes being discovered. On the basis of these facts, the Dutch scholar B. Haak gives a new interpretation to the inscription on this painting: *Rembrandt verandert En over geschildert. 1636* (Rembrandt altered and repainted. 1636). He suggests that the inscription be read: "Rembrandt changed (in comparison to the preceding version) and painted anew", in other words, he believes the painting to be a Rembrandt original. However, it was not the inscription alone that gave scholars reason to consider the Munich painting the work of a pupil, done after his master's drawing and corrected by him. The evidence of many weak and flabby lines and of the poor draughtsmanship also corroborates this theory (some scholars attribute this work with certainty to Govaert Flinck).

The canvas has been replaced, as testified to by the following inscription in Russian on the reverse side: "Transferred from the old to the new canvas in St Petersburg by F. Tabuntsov in 1850." Restored breaks are apparent at the top to the right and at the bottom to the left. Numerous old overpaintings can be traced along the horizontal seam and above Abraham's head. Some inpaintings are visible on Isaac's elbow, loin and foot, as well as on the thicket to the left and on the background.

PROVENANCE:

1760	September 16: on sale in Amsterdam, lot No 1 (bought by de Winter for 100 florins)
1767	Robert Walpole Collection, Houghton Hall, England
1779	Acquired for the Hermitage

EXHIBITIONS:

1936	Rembrandt. Moscow—Leningrad (Cat., p. 44, No 8)
1956	Rembrandt and His School. Moscow—Leningrad (Cat., pp. 51—52)
1968	Masterpieces of Rembrandt. Tokyo—Kioto (Cat. No 5)
1969	Rembrandt 1669—1969. Amsterdam (Cat. No 4a)
1969—70	Rembrandt, His Precursors and Followers. Leningrad (Cat., p. 21, No 8)
1973	Caravaggio and His Followers. Leningrad (Cat. No 42)

LITERATURE:

Имп. Эрмитаж 1863—1916, № 792; Bode 1873, S. 13; Bode 1883, S. 431; Valentiner 1909, S. 170; Hofstede de Groot, 1915, Nr. 9; К. Фолль, *Опыт сравнительного изучения картин*, Петроград, 1916, с. 179; K. Baudissin, «Rembrandt und Cats», *Repertorium für Kunstwissenschaft*, 45, 1925, S. 152—154; Weisbach 1926, S. 63, 188; K. Müller, «Studien zu Lastman und Rembrandt», *Jahrbuch der preußischen Kunstsammlungen*, 50, 1929, S. 64—67; Benesch 1935, S. 18; Rosenberg 1948, p. 105, 225; Hamann 1948, S. 249, 259—261; Knuttel 1956, blz. 93; Левинсон-Лессинг 1956, с. VIII; Гос. Эрмитаж 1958, с. 252; Фехнер 1965, № 9; J. W. von Moltke, *Govaert Flinck*, Amsterdam, 1965, p. 13; E. Brochhagen, B. Knuttel, *Holländische Malerei des 17. Jahrhunderts. Alte Pinakothek, München. Katalog 3*, München, 1967, S. 72—75; Gerson 1968, No 74; Haak 1968, blz. 126; W. Stechow, "Some Observations on Rembrandt and Lastman", *Oud-Holland*, LXXXIV, 1969, blz. 150; Bredius, No 498.

Salomon Koninck. Parable of the Labourers in the
Vineyard. The Hermitage, Leningrad

11. PARABLE OF THE LABOURERS IN THE VINEYARD

Oil on oak, cradled. 31 × 42 cm
Signed and dated at bottom, right: *Rembrandt f. 1637*
The Hermitage, Leningrad. No 757

The Gospel parable (*Matthew*, 20. 1—16) which served as the subject for this painting tells
the story of the householder who hired several groups of labourers for his vineyard during
the course of the day, from early morning until "the eleventh hour". When night was come
he paid them all the same wages, causing those who had worked from the very morning to
"murmur against the goodman of the house". The idea of the parable is that all are equal
before God.
The particular aspect of the interpretation on Rembrandt's part is that, while depicting the
scene of payment, he put special stress on the demands of the dissatisfied labourers. Three
personages, the householder and two labourers, not only occupy the central place and are
flooded by the brightest light, but are given the most complete treatment by the artist.
The content of Rembrandt's painting has attracted the attention of many students of his art,
as well as of those interested in the iconography of the subject. In his well-known work, *De
iconografie van de contra-reformatie in de Nederlanden*, B. Knipping states that Rembrandt
"turned the scene of payment into a real-life business transaction". R. Hamann defines the
picture's content even more concretely: "The painting as a whole gives the impression of
a wealthy Amsterdam trader's office." It is interesting to note that as early as the eighteenth
century a French engraving of this work bore the title *The Amsterdam Merchant*.
To our mind, however, Rembrandt's painting transcends the limits of a genre scene; it may
have reflected certain events that took place in Leyden, the painter's natal city, in the year

Parable of the Labourers in the Vineyard. Detail (X-ray photograph).
The Hermitage, Leningrad

of the painting's creation. "The dominating atmosphere of the Leyden textile works," writes E. Baasch, "was characterized by the apprentices' urge to unite at a very early stage and make a common effort to defend their rights. In 1637 there were even several strikes."

Thus it was that through the evangelic tale Rembrandt was able to depict a theme of great social significance. The painting's actual content, whatever the artist's intention, did not only outgrow the parable *per se*, but even came into serious contradiction with it. For if Rembrandt had been faithful to the Gospel episode, he would have had to show that the labourers were at fault, while the householder was in his right. In reality, the painter's sympathies are clearly on the side of the men.

The concealed symbolic content of the painting, as we see it, confirms this interpretation. I the centre of the canvas the painter depicted a cat and a mouse caught in its paws. The Dutch popular saying "to lead a cat-and-mouse life", besides underlining the traditional element of enmity, also conveys the cat's tyranny. It is in this sense that it was used as legend on the medal commemorating the events of the Dutch revolution.

The Gospel parable continued to attract Rembrandt in subsequent years. Besides a second painting, which cannot be attributed to the painter's brush with final certainty, being known only through Amsterdam auctions of 1803 and 1829, there are many drawings on this subject dating to the forties and fifties of the seventeenth century.

Rembrandt's painting became the decisive factor in the subject's iconographic treatment in Dutch art, not only by his own pupils and followers, such as S. van Hoogstraten, J. Victors, G. van Eeckhout, Philipps and Salomon Koninck, but by other masters in no way connected with Rembrandt, for instance, H. M. Sorgh. Besides the painting's theme directly touching the issues of the day, its popularity can be explained by traits that bind it to the typically Dutch small-size, interior genre scene. However, the problems of this type of painting are solved here on a supreme level of mastery. The light pouring through the windows and dimming in the background seems to fill the interior with air. This serves to unite all aspects and details of the picture: the central group, the scribe, the workers, and the domestic bric-à-brac that clutters up the room. The domination of tone over colour, the decisive importance of *valeurs*, so characteristic of Dutch painting of the thirties and forties, find its most perfect embodiment in this canvas.

X-ray study shows that the first version had one more window, which the artist painted out in the process of work.

The picture, done in very liquid paint (sometimes the technique resembles that of the grisaille), is in good condition. The X-rays show a thick layer of white applied only to the blue sky, visible through the window openings. The areas where ultramarine is mixed with other pigments (the group of workers in the background and the window curtains) have suffered from ultramarine decomposition.

PROVENANCE:

Until 1740   Collection of Pierre Crozat, Paris
Until 1750   Collection of François Crozat, Baron du Châtel, Paris
Until 1772   Collection of Crozat, Baron de Thiers, Paris
     1772   Acquired for the Hermitage

EXHIBITIONS:

1936   Rembrandt. Moscow—Leningrad (Cat., p. 45, No 11)
1956   Rembrandt and His School. Moscow—Leningrad (Cat., p. 53)
1969—70   Rembrandt, His Precursors and Followers. Leningrad (Cat., pp. 23—24, No 10)

LITERATURE:

Имп. Эрмитаж 1863—1916, № 798; Bode 1873, S. 13; Bode 1883, S. 446; Valentiner 1909, S. 183; Hofstede de Groot 1915, Nr 116; Weisbach 1926, S. 151—152; Benesch 1935, S. 26; B. Knipping, *De iconografie van de contra-reformatie in de Nederlanden*, Hilversum, 1939, d. I, blz. 301; Hamann 1948, S. 264—266; Левинсон-Лессинг 1956, с. IX; Виппер 1957, с. 317; Гос. Эрмитаж 1958, с. 252; Ю. Кузнецов, «Картина Рембрандта *Притча о работниках на винограднике*», *Труды Государственного Эрмитажа*, VI, 1961, с. 60—87; Levinson-Lessing 1964, No 76; Фехнер 1965, № 11; Bauch 1966, Nr 65; Gerson 1968, No 83; Bredius, No 558.

The Frame-maker Herman Doomer.
1640. Metropolitan Museum
of Art, New York

12. PORTRAIT OF BAERTJEN MARTENS DOOMER

Oil on oak, cradled. 76 × 56 cm
Signed on the background at bottom, left: *Rebrandt f.* (sic!)
The Hermitage, Leningrad. No 721

In 1909 W. Martin identified the woman in the portrait as Baertjen Doomer, the wife of Rembrandt's frame-maker and mother of Lambert Doomer (1622—1700), Rembrandt's pupil, later a landscape painter. In 1640, Rembrandt painted the portrait of her husband Herman Doomer (Metropolitan Museum of Art, New York, Bredius 217). The companion portrait of his wife was probably painted in the same year.

In this portrait Rembrandt created an amazingly natural and attractive image of a simple woman. The intimate character and special warmth make the portrait, together with its pendant, stand apart from the commissioned portraits of that period. Baertjen dressed in all her finery to sit for Rembrandt. The kind and pleasant expression of her face and eyes, the smile that seems to flit across her features, cannot hide her embarrassment at sitting for such a famous master. Interesting to note, in the first version of the portrait, as X-ray study showed, Baertjen held a crumpled handkerchief in her hand. Later, Rembrandt eliminated this detail which distracted the viewer's attention.

This portrait may also be regarded as one of the first examples of the artist's turning to chiaroscuro as a means of showing the model's inner world. In the 1630s the painter knew how to contrast areas of light and shadow to stress the dramatic content of his compositions; now, moving toward psychological portrayal, his painting features subtle, almost imperceptible transitions from light to shadow, with the appliance of semitransparent glazed strokes. In the *Portrait of Baertjen Martens Doomer* the airy, translucent shadows that flit across the woman's face,

Portrait of Baertjen Martens Doomer. Hands (X-ray photograph).
The Hermitage, Leningrad

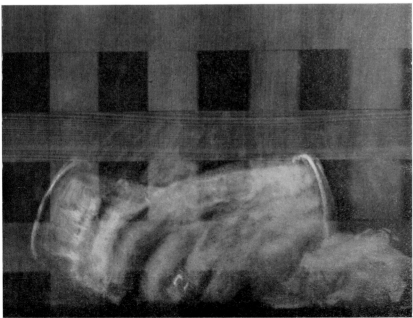

the light reflected from her white collar onto her cheeks and chin, and the vibrating, glowing atmosphere that softly envelops her figure, seem to constantly change the expression of her eyes and mouth.

On June 23, 1662, Baertjen, already a widow, drew up her will in which she states her desire that "...her son Lambert Doomer receive and keep her portrait, and that of her husband, painted by Rembrandt, but only on condition that his brothers and sisters be given copies of these portraits, the cost of which he will pay..." These conditions were carried out, and five copies of the two portraits were made for the other brothers and sisters. Some of these copies have reached us. Among them the portraits of Lambert's parents, bearing the name of Rembrandt and belonging to the collection of the Duke of Devonshire, cannot be considered as copies because they differ greatly from the Rembrandt originals.

The present condition of the picture is as follows: the upper left and the lower right corners of the panel were damaged and then restored. Discernible near the bonnet is overpainting done by the artist to make it smaller. On the background, left, numerous overpaintings can be traced along the priming losses which left the wooden panel exposed.

PROVENANCE:

1640	Herman Doomer Collection, Amsterdam
1654	Baertjen Doomer Collection, Amsterdam
1678	Lambert Doomer Collection, Amsterdam
1700	Collection of Herman Foster Jr., nephew of Lambert Doomer who bequeathed the portrait to him, Amsterdam
1797	Acquired for the Hermitage

EXHIBITIONS:

1936	Rembrandt. Moscow—Leningrad (Cat., p. 45, No 12)
1956	Rembrandt. Amsterdam—Rotterdam (Cat., p. 89, No 42)
1969—70	Rembrandt, His Precursors and Followers. Leningrad (Cat., p. 25, No 12)

LITERATURE:

Имп. Эрмитаж 1863—1916, № 829; Bode 1873, S. 9; Hofstede de Groot 1897—1905, Beil., Nr 251a; Valentiner 1909, S. 255; W. Martin, «Rembrandt's portret van Herman Doomer en Baertjen Martens», *Bulletin van de Nederlands oudheidkondigen Bond*, 2, 1909, blz. 126—129; A. Bredius, «Rembrandtiana», *Oud-Holland*, XXVIII, 1910, blz. 2—18; Hofstede de Groot 1915, Nr 643; Knuttel 1956, blz. 118; Левинсон-Лессинг 1956, c. IX; I. H. van Eeghen, «Baertjen Martens en Herman Doomer», *Maandblad Amstelodamum*, 43, 1956, blz. 133; Гос. Эрмитаж 1958, c. 252; Виппер 1962, c. 350; Фехнер 1965, № 14; Bauch 1966, Nr 499; Gerson 1968, No 231; Haak 1968, blz. 166; Bredius, No 357.

The Return of the Prodigal Son. Drawing.
Teyler Museum, Haarlem

13. DAVID'S FAREWELL TO JONATHAN

Oil on oak, cradled. 73 × 61 cm
Signed and dated at bottom centre: *Rembrandt f. 1642*
The Hermitage, Leningrad. No 713

The canvas, by all probabilities, depicts an episode from the Bible: young David, whose life
is threatened by King Saul, bids farewell to the King's son, his friend Jonathan. The Bible
gives a moving description of this final moment of farewell: "and they kissed one another, and
wept one with another, until David exceeded" (*1 Samuel*, 20. 41).

For many years Rembrandt scholars tried to interpret the painting's subject, but to this day
they have not reached any conclusion that could be regarded as universally accepted. In old
Hermitage inventories the picture was entered as the *Return of the Prodigal Son* (1797, 1859), then
as the *Reconciliation of Esau and Jacob* (*Genesis*, 33. 4). This latter interpretation was accepted
without much discussion and was frequently referred to in literature during the nineteenth century. It was A. Somov who made a critical analysis of this when working on the Hermitage
catalogue of 1893. Somov suggested that the painting depicted the reconciliation of David and
Absalom after the latter had killed his brother Amnon (*2 Samuel*, 14. 33). After examining
all the possible biblical connotations of this scene, Hofstede de Groot came to the same conclusion in 1923.

In 1925 K. Baudissin suggested that Rembrandt's painting depicts the parting of David and
Jonathan. For evidence he points to the quiver and arrows Jonathan used to warn David of
Saul's wrath (lower right-hand corner), and the stone Ezel, where they met, according to the
text of the Bible. But he could find no explanation for David's royal apparel, and his version
was therefore not accepted. In 1957 V. Loewinson-Lessing published an article that cleared up
the matter. In Chapter 18 (not 20), 1—5, of the First Book of Samuel, it is said that Jonathan,
loving David, "stripped himself of the robe that was upon him, and gave it to David, and his
garments, even to his sword, and to his bow, and to his girdle". The entrance to David's
secret hiding-place, depicted in the far right, to our belief confirms this hypothesis: David
waited there for Jonathan during three days.

V. Loewinson-Lessing was able to find yet another important corroboration of the new inter-
pretation. He discovered archival data showing that the painting was bought for Peter the
Great in Amsterdam by one Osip Solovyov at an auction of Jan van Beuningen's collection on
May 13, 1716; the painting was entitled *David and Jonathan*.

Since 1957 the new interpretation has been accepted by the majority of scholars. Only Jakob
Rosenberg and J. van Regteren Altena doubt it; the latter believes that the man resembling
Rembrandt is too old for Jonathan. Although H. Gerson continues to call the painting by its
old name in both his monograph and the revised Bredius edition, he notes that "the iconographic details of the painting are in complete accordance with the farewell episode of the
two friends".

Among the few Rembrandt drawings that repeat this or similar scenes, the closest to the Hermitage painting is the drawing *The Return of the Prodigal Son* (Teyler Museum, Haarlem,
Benesch 519), now also dated 1642. Professor J. van Gelder quite correctly believes it to be
the prototype for the Hermitage painting.

J. van Gelder voices yet another suggestion which, to our mind, is especially noteworthy. In
a promissory note of March 1659 Rembrandt took upon himself the completion in one year's
time of a painting already under way, entitled *David and Jonathan*, to be subsequently given

as a repayment of debt to his creditor, the Amsterdam merchant Lodowijck van Ludick. Seeing certain parallels in the colour range between the Hermitage painting and the works of the 1660s, J. van Gelder suggests that the 1642 canvas was possibly greatly altered by the artist two decades later, which explains its appearance in the note of 1659. Visual study and X-ray investigation have not uncovered any substantial changes in the colour scheme, but all the same van Gelder may be right in his presumption.

Three splices measuring 11 by 13 cm, 1.9 by 2.2 cm and 2.6 by 2.7 cm were inserted by the painter into the upper part of the panel, its right-hand corner being seriously damaged. Numerous, sometimes darkened overpaintings can be traced over the old fractures of the panel and the vertical cracks (also at the top of the picture). Light brown overpaintings are also apparent in the right part of the picture, on the stone portal of the secret hiding-place.

The sky is done in very liquid paint revealing almost everywhere the white priming. Rather high impasto is applied only to the figures (see the X-ray photograph). The author's corrections are visible in the area around Jonathan's head and in the lower part of the architectural setting partially covered with the bushes added later. A curtain at the entrance to the hiding-place was originally seen more distinctly in the upper right-hand corner.

Mentioning the unfinished *David and Jonathan* in 1659, Rembrandt may have had in mind the Hermitage picture, which needed some patching-up. There is yet another evidence in favour of this argument: no other Rembrandt painting on this subject has been discovered, probably due to the fact that none existed.

PROVENANCE:

1659	March: the painting is probably the one mentioned in the promissory note signed by Rembrandt to Lodowijck van Ludick in Amsterdam
1678	October 19: was probably mentioned in the post-mortem inventory of Herman Becker in Amsterdam
1713	April 19: was on sale with the collection of L. van der Heem in Amsterdam (sold for 105 florins)
1716	May 13: was on sale with the collection of Jan van Beuningen (sold for 80 florins)
1716	May 13: acquired for Peter the Great in Amsterdam for 80 florins by Osip Solovyov and sent to St Petersburg on June 19 of that year, where it was subsequently displayed in the Monplaisir Palace at Peterhof
1882	Transferred from the Monplaisir Palace to the Hermitage

David's Farewell to Jonathan. Detail (X-ray photograph).
The Hermitage, Leningrad

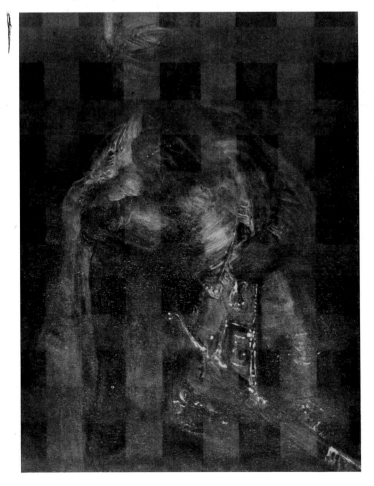

EXHIBITIONS:

1936   Rembrandt. Moscow—Leningrad (Cat., p. 45, No 13)
1956   Rembrandt. Amsterdam—Rotterdam (Cat., p. 97, No 46)
1969—70   Rembrandt, His Precursors and Followers. Leningrad (Cat., p. 24, No 11)

LITERATURE:

А. Васильчиков, «Новые приобретения Императорского Эрмитажа», *Вестник изящных искусств*, 1883, I, с. 25; Bode 1883, S. 44; Сомов 1893, № 1777; Valentiner 1909, S. 227; Hofstede de Groot 1915, Nr 38; K. Baudissin, «Anmerkungen zu Rembrandt-Erklärung», *Repertorium für Kunstwissenschaft*, 46, 1925, S. 190—192; Weisbach 1926, S. 219, 317; Benesch 1935, S. 30; Hamann 1948, S. 268—269; Левинсон-Лессинг 1956, с. X—XI; Knuttel 1956, blz. 144; J. Rosenberg, «Die Rembrandt-Ausstellungen in Holland», *Kunstchronik*, Dezember 1956, S. 346; W. R. Valentiner, *Art Quarterly*, 19, 1956, p. 395; J. Rosenberg, *Art Quarterly*, 19, 1956, p. 383; J. van Gelder, H. Gerson, H. Kauffmann, J. Q. van Regteren Altena, *Kunstchronik*, Mai 1957, S. 146; В. Ф. Левинсон-Лессинг, «К истории картины Рембрандта *Давид и Ионафан*», *Сообщения Государственного Эрмитажа*, XI, 1957, с. 5—8; Гос. Эрмитаж 1958, с. 256; А. Членов, «К вопросу о сюжете картины Рембрандта *Давид и Урия*», *Искусство*, 1958, № 10, с. 60—61; Виппер 1962, с. 347, 507—508, прим. 124; Levinson-Lessing 1964, Nos 77, 78; Фехнер 1965, № 13; Вольская 1966, с. 64; Bauch 1966, Nr 24; Gerson 1968, No 207; Bredius, No 511; Ch. Tümpel, «Studien zur Ikonographie der Historien Rembrandts», *Nederlands kunsthistorisch Jaarboek*, XX, 1969, blz. 140—146.

14. PORTRAIT OF AN OLD MAN

Oil on oak, cradled. 51 × 42 cm (enlarged on all sides by later additions); original dimensions: 47 × 37 cm
Signed with a monogram right, above the shoulder: *R. f.*
The Hermitage, Leningrad. No 755

Judging by the craquelures, the background was repainted in the eighteenth century. The face, however, was left almost untouched, which allows for both artistic evaluation and dating: about 1643. Aged people's faces fascinated Rembrandt throughout his creative life. But if in the early 1630s these were physiognomistic studies, in which the artist experimented in conveying facial expressions, it is possible to qualify a group of portrait studies of the 1640s as psychological. The Hermitage *Portrait of an Old Man* is one of their most striking examples.
The sorrowful expression of the eyes and face of the man is accentuated by the gesture of the right hand resting over his heart. The genre motivation of an inner state was introduced with a view to simplifying the artistic problem. The gesture plays no really important role and can be "read" only together with the expression of the face. Such studies are an important stage along the way to Rembrandt's psychological portraits of the two following decades.
Hofstede de Groot mentions three copies of this picture which, in his time, were part of the Count Brownlow collection in Esbridge Park (spuriously signed and dated 1632), the Earl of Carlisle collection in Noworth, England, and the Wedewer collection in Wiesbaden, auctioned at Cologne on May 1, 1899 (lot 17, as the work of Ferdinand Bol).
The existence of three copies of a portrait, the model of which could not *per se* warrant copying, makes one suppose they were done as pupils' studies. Perhaps Rembrandt's students were assigned such work in order that they should learn to grasp the complex mechanism of the model's inner world.

PROVENANCE:

1852	Collection of the Count of Morgny, Paris; May 24: sold in Paris for 8,000 francs
1852	Acquired for the Hermitage

EXHIBITIONS:

1936	Rembrandt. Moscow—Leningrad (Cat., p. 45, No 15)
1956	Rembrandt and His School. Moscow—Leningrad (Cat., p. 55)
1969—70	Rembrandt, His Precursors and Followers. Leningrad (Cat., p. 26, No 14)

LITERATURE:

Имп. Эрмитаж 1863—1916, № 815; Valentiner 1909, S. 358; Hofstede de Groot 1915, Nr 437; Benesch 1935, S. 37; Левинсон-Лессинг 1956, с. XIII; Фехнер 1965, № 16; Bauch 1966, Nr 183; Gerson 1968, No 242; Bredius, No 229.

The Holy Family Sleeping. *Ca.* 1645. Drawing.
The L. Clark Collection, Cambridge (Mass.)

Infant in a Cradle. *Ca.* 1645. Drawing.
Present location unknown

15. THE HOLY FAMILY WITH ANGELS

Oil on canvas, relined. 117 × 91 cm
Signed and dated at bottom, left: *Rembrandt f. 1645*
The Hermitage, Leningrad. No 741

In the 1640s Rembrandt painted several canvases on the Holy Family theme. The Hermitage painting represents his supreme achievement.

The Gospel subject is of such a genre interpretation as to make one want to call it *The Carpenter's Family*. Even the group of angels does not lessen the real-life impression. And yet, Rembrandt's *Holy Family* is not a mere genre scene, so typical of Dutch art. The painting is poetic and pregnant with a deeply lyrical feeling. The theme of a mother's love, a subject of such attraction to so many artists, besides a human and sincere quality, acquires a lofty aspect under Rembrandt's brush.

Studies from nature preceded the painting of the Hermitage canvas, as was usually the case with Rembrandt. Perhaps Hendrickje Stoffels served as Mary's model. Hendrickje was a young peasant girl who entered the painter's household as a servant and later became his mistress and faithful companion. Three Rembrandt drawings have been preserved, all of which undoubtedly pertain to the Hermitage painting. One is a general compositional sketch (L. Clark collection, Cambridge, Mass., Benesch 569), where the entire Holy Family is shown sleeping. Perhaps the drawing shows the moment before the Holy Family fled into Egypt, known in iconography as St Joseph's vision. But if that is the case, only one angel should appear, instead of several, to warn Joseph about the danger that threatens the Infant Christ. This is in accordance with the scene represented on Rembrandt's canvas dated 1645, now in the Dahlem Museum, Berlin (Bredius 569). In the Clark collection drawing we have a detailed study, something very close to the Hermitage painting: the cradle with the sleeping infant and the group of angels. The general compositional sketch of the Hermitage painting is in the Musée Bonnat, Bayonne (Bredius 567). Finally, in the former collection of H. Oppenheimer, there was a study of a cradle with a sleeping infant, exactly identical to the Hermitage painting, except that it was the mirror-reflection version.

The Holy Family at the Carpenter's Workshop.
Ca. 1645. Drawing. Musée Bonnat, Bayonne

The *Head of a Young Girl* (a private USA collection, Bredius 375), which was formerly considered to be a study for the Hermitage painting, is in reality, as suggested by H. Gerson, only a partial copy made by the master's pupils.

A 2.5 cm wide strip at the top and a 1.5 cm wide hidden strip at the bottom are later additions. In a number of places, mainly on the background and on Joseph's and Mary's dress, there are overpaintings covering the most obvious craquelures. The painter's corrections are apparent on the kerchief and on the breast of Mary.

PROVENANCE:

1733	Perhaps on sale at the auction of the Adriaen Bout Collection at The Hague
Until 1740	Collection of Pierre Crozat, Paris
Until 1750	Collection of François Crozat, Baron du Châtel, Paris
Until 1772	Collection of Crozat, Baron de Thiers, Paris
1772	Acquired for the Hermitage

EXHIBITIONS:

1936	Rembrandt. Moscow—Leningrad (Cat., p. 45, No 16)
1956	Rembrandt. Amsterdam—Rotterdam (Cat., p. 105, No 50)
1969—70	Rembrandt, His Precursors and Followers. Leningrad (Cat., p. 26, No 15)

LITERATURE:

Имп. Эрмитаж 1863—1916, № 796; Bode 1873, S. 14—15; Bode 1883, S. 476; Valentiner 1909, S. 281; Hofstede de Groot 1915, Nr 94; Weisbach 1926, S. 154, 156; Benesch 1935, S. 36—37; Hamann 1948, S. 287, 289; Rosenberg 1948, pp. 51, 121—122; Левинсон-Лессинг 1956, с. XI; Knuttel 1956, blz. 145, 146; Виппер 1962, с. 366, 374—375; Levinson-Lessing 1964, Nos 79, 80; Фехнер 1965, № 17; Bauch 1966, Nr 73; Gerson 1968, No 211; Haak 1968, blz. 188—189; Bredius, No 570.

Old Woman Seated in an Armchair.
Ca. 1643. Drawing.
The Count A. Seylern Collection, London

16. PORTRAIT OF AN OLD WOMAN WITH SPECTACLES

Oil on oak, cradled. 61 × 49 cm
Signed and dated right of centre, on the wall: *Rembrandt f. 1643*
The Hermitage, Leningrad. No 759

This painting belongs to those rare works of Rembrandt, the preparatory studies for which have been preserved. In the Count Seylern collection in London there is a black chalk drawing done in the energetic bold manner of the 1630s and early 1640s (Benesch 684). It depicts a woman in identical dress and sitting in the same pose. The hands and spectacles are absent in the drawing, as well as all decorative elements of the dress. The main changes, however, are in the facial expression — the element of will-power, so evident in the drawing, disappears in the picture.

The sitter in both cases is reminiscent of the 1639 oval portrait called *Rembrandt's Mother* (Kunsthistorisches Museum, Vienna, Bredius 71). The clothes are similar in both portraits, although the headdress is closer to the resplendent shawl covering the woman's head in the painting at Windsor Castle (Bredius 70). In what concerns the old woman's pose and the composition of the painting as a whole, the nearest analogy is the etching *Rembrandt's Mother at the Table* (Bartsch 343). This similarity made Wilhelm Bode voice his support of the traditional title of *Rembrandt's Mother*, which, however, was not accepted by subsequent scholars. Bode believed the date 1643 to be a falsification and considered the portrait to have been produced around 1639, the date of the Vienna picture.

W. R. Valentiner's attempt to identify the woman as Titus's nurse Geertge Dircx was also refuted. It is hard to agree with those who suggest that the painting should be called *Old Prophetess* (K. Bauch) or *Anna the Prophetess* (Ch. Tümpel), since portraits of that period are nearer to genre paintings than to biblical "histories".

More noteworthy, to our mind, is the attempt of G. Knuttel to give the picture its traditional title and consider it as the post-mortem portrait of the painter's mother, Neeltje Willemsdochter Gerritzoon (married 1589, died 1640). Let us recall that Rembrandt painted the post-mortem portrait of Saskia in 1643 (Dahlem Museum, Berlin, Bredius 109). There is really nothing strange in the fact that portraits based on memory differ slightly from those painted from nature (a life study, made somewhat earlier, probably served for the Hermitage painting).

Compared to other Rembrandt's paintings based on a previous careful study of the sitter, his *Old Woman with Spectacles* is somewhat flabby. This impression, however, may be due to the thick coat of dirty varnish under which the author's alterations and old overpaintings are visible. The right background was originally painted with transparent browns followed by greenish-greys which concealed both signature and date. Numerous overpaintings in black are visible on the apparel. In the area around the head there are some corrections intended to reduce the dimensions of the headdress which in the first version corresponded to the preparatory drawing. Similar corrections are visible on the forehead; they changed the kerchief line which originally had been painted much lower, in approximately the same way as on the drawing. Overpaintings applied to the face are most distinct in the lower part of the right cheek. Was it the master's hand that made the changes, or the hand of some other painter? At present no definite answer can be given. Final judgment must be withheld until after cleaning in regard to authenticity, too, which recently has been questioned. For the same reasons we can neither accept nor refute H. Gerson's suggestion that the painting is the work of one of Rembrandt's pupils, perhaps Abraham van Dijck.

PROVENANCE:

Until 1767   De Julienne Collection, Paris; March 20: sold for 3,401 francs
      1767   Acquired for the Hermitage

EXHIBITIONS:

1936   Rembrandt. Moscow—Leningrad (Cat., p. 45, No 14)
1956   Rembrandt and His School. Moscow—Leningrad (Cat., p. 54)
1969—70   Rembrandt, His Precursors and Followers. Leningrad (Cat., pp. 25—26, No 13)

LITERATURE:

Имп. Эрмитаж 1863—1916, № 807; Bode 1873, S. 9; Valentiner 1909, S. 250; Hofstede de Groot 1915, Nr 319; Benesch 1935, S. 33; Knuttel 1956, blz. 139; Гос. Эрмитаж 1958, c. 256; Фехнер 1965, № 15; Bauch 1966, Nr 267; Bredius, No 361; Ch. Tümpel, «Studien zur Ikonographie der Historien Rembrandts», *Nederlands kunsthistorisch Jaarboek*, XX, 1969, blz. 178—180.

Rembrandt (?). Danaë. 1630s. Drawing.
Herzog Anton Ulrich Museum,
Brunswick

Saskia Wearing Pearls. 1634. Etching

17. DANAË

Oil on canvas, relined. 185 × 203 cm
Signed and dated at bottom, left: *Rembrandt. f. 1636* (the date is difficult to read)
The Hermitage, Leningrad. No 723

The picture is based on a mythological subject that attracted many painters. Danaë's father Acrisius, the King of Argos, was forewarned that he would be killed by his daughter's son; therefore he imprisoned Danaë in a tower. Enamoured of her, Zeus (Jupiter) entered the tower in the form of a shower of gold. The depiction of the golden rain was considered obligatory in the interpretation of this legend. The absence of it in Rembrandt's painting led to doubts concerning the subject of the canvas. The first to voice his doubts was J. Smith in 1836. He called Rembrandt's painting *Awaiting Her Lover*. Since then eleven fundamentally different hypotheses have been advanced. W. Bode (1873 and 1883) and N. Chechulin (1912) believed the young woman to be the biblical Sarah, the daughter of Raguel, waiting for Tobias; A. Jordan (1884) and W. Niemeyer (1931) suggested she was Hagar to whom Sarah brought her

Danaë. Head (X-ray photograph). The Hermitage, Leningrad

Danaë. Right hand (X-ray photograph). The Hermitage, Leningrad

husband Abraham; R. Wustmann (1909—10) and H. von Kauffmann (1920) said she was the wife of the Roman Emperor Claudius, Messalina; J. van Dycke (1923) decided she was Potiphar's wife trying to seduce Joseph; K. von Baudissin (1925) and A. Chlenov (1960) qualified her as Bathsheba waiting for David; W. Drost (1926), as Dalilah tempting Samson; W. Weisbach (1926), as Venus awaiting Mars; S. Rosenthal (1928), as Rachel waiting for Jacob; C. Brière-Misme (1952—54), as Leah waiting for Jacob; N. MacLaren (1960), as Semele awaiting Jupiter. The traditional interpretation was upheld by E. Panofsky (1933), as well as by the authors of official Hermitage editions. Recent investigations and stylistic analysis led to very important discoveries in the iconographic motifs; they furnished the clue to the problem of the painting's subject (see note to p. 19 of the present edition).

Here are the most significant alterations introduced into the picture:

1. The position of Danaë's right arm and hand has been changed. The hand and arm, as we see them today, were completely repainted by the author. In the first version, the right hand and arm were slightly lower than now, and the palm was turned down, not outward and forward. X-ray plates also showed an airy white draping that covered Danaë's hips. The lower end of this draping, lying on Danaë's hip, was painted in thick strokes discernible to the naked eye. Danaë held the upper end in her right hand. Hence, her hand lifted the draping from her hips, at the same time, as might be supposed by the position of her palm, pushing aside the curtains of the bed.

2. Danaë's head has been completely repainted, her features and hairdo changed. The first Danaë was more snub-nosed and her face was rounder, in other words, she had a greater likeness

Danaë. Left hand (X-ray photograph). The Hermitage, Leningrad

Danaë. Legs (X-ray photograph). The Hermitage, Leningrad

to Saskia than to the present Danaë. X-ray plates also showed her to have been looking more upward. This is a very important discovery, for it confirms the supposition that in the first version Rembrandt followed the prescribed tradition. Finally, Danaë's neck and ears were decorated with twin strings of pearls and large earrings that the artist later painted out.

3. Danaë's right leg was much more definitely bent in the knee.

4. On the bed-table there were several pieces of jewellery (the string of beads hanging from the table is visible to the naked eye).

5. X-rays of the painting's upper left-hand part show the first version's position of the old woman-servant. She was placed much further to the left, depicted in strict profile, and was also looking upward. The bed curtain that the old woman now pulls aside was extended to the left, and the space under the canopy, now so large and of such compositional importance, was a mere narrow strip.

Alterations, as the X-ray results showed, affected not only the composition, but also the colour scheme and the manner of execution. The golden tone and free style of the central area are due to later changes. These data allowed to reconsider the history of the work on the painting and to establish two distinctly separate periods of its creation, i.e. 1636 and 1646—47.

In 1636, when Danaë was painted from Saskia, Rembrandt most powerfully expressed the realistic aspect of life by depicting a naked female body, with the classical concept of beauty very strongly felt. In 1646—47, with Geertge Dircx as Danaë, Rembrandt conveyed primarily the aesthetic worth of the inner, spiritual world.

The picture's condition is good. Besides the usual crumblings along the edges, there are two considerable losses of paint and priming painted out later: under the pillow and on the bed-

Danaë. Table (X-ray photograph). The Hermitage, Leningrad

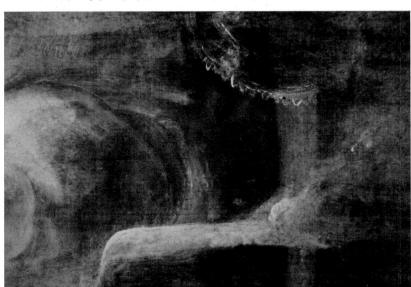

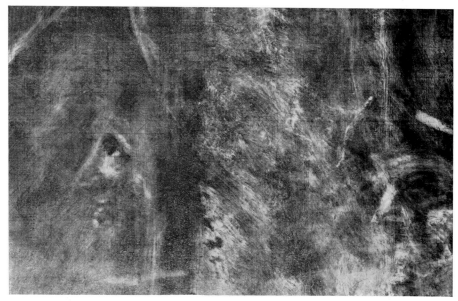

Danaë. Old woman-servant (X-ray photograph). The Hermitage, Leningrad

spread below Danaë's shins. The ultraviolet plate shows restoration retouching applied to the lower part of the belly and to the right hip of Danaë, as well as to the old woman-servant's head.

PROVENANCE:

Until 1740   Collection of Pierre Crozat, Paris
Until 1750   Collection of François Crozat, Baron du Châtel, Paris
Until 1772   Collection of Crozat, Baron de Thiers, Paris
        1772   Acquired for the Hermitage

EXHIBITIONS:

1936   Rembrandt. Moscow—Leningrad (Cat., p. 44, No 10)
1956   Rembrandt and His School. Moscow—Leningrad (Cat., p. 52)

Danaë. Cupid (X-ray photograph). The Hermitage, Leningrad

1969—70   Rembrandt, His Precursors and Followers. Leningrad (Cat., pp. 21—22, No 9)
1978   Rembrandt. *Danaë*. Tokyo (Cat. No 1)

LITERATURE:

John Smith, *A Catalogue Raisonné of the Works of the Most Eminent Dutch... Painters*, London, 1863, vol. VII, No 173; Имп. Эрмитаж 1863—1916, № 802; Bode 1873, S. 13—14; H. Riegel, *Die niederländischen Schulen im Herzoglichen Museum zu Braunschweig*, Berlin, 1882, S. 258; Bode 1883, S. 449—451; A. Jordan, «Bemerkungen zu einigen Bildern Rembrandts», *Repertorium für Kunstwissenschaft*, 1884, S. 85; Valentiner 1909, S. 176; R. Wustmann, *Bühne und Welt*, XII, 1909/1910, S. 182; Н. Чечулин, «Что изображено на картине Рембрандта, известной под именем *Данаи*», *Старые годы*, 1912, VI, с. 39—42; Hofstede de Groot 1915, Nr 197; Hans von Kauffmann, «Rembrandt und die Humanisten von Muidenkring», *Jahrbuch der preußischen Kunstsammlungen*, 1920, S. 61, 65; John C. van Dycke, *Rembrandt and His School*, New York, 1923, p. 104; K. Baudissin, «Rembrandt und Cats», *Repertorium für Kunstwissenschaft*, 45, 1925, S. 160 ff.; W. Drost, *Barockmalerei in den germanischen Ländern*, Wildpark—Potsdam, 1926, S. 159; Weisbach 1926, S. 242—244; S. Rosenthal, «Neue Deutungen von Historienbildern aus dem Rembrandtskreis», *Jahrbuch für Kunstwissenschaft*, 1928, S. 105—110; W. Niemeyer, «Rembrandts Danae ist Hagar», *Repertorium für Kunstwissenschaft*, 52, 1931, S. 61—62; E. Panofsky, «Der gefesselte Eros (Zur Genealogie von Rembrandts *Danae*)», *Oud-Holland*, LVl, 1933, blz. 193—217; Benesch 1935, S. 18; Hamann 1948, S. 45—46, 66, 95, 228; Rosenberg 1948, S. 53, 161—164, 176, 198; C. Brière-Misme, «La *Danaë* de Rembrandt et son véritable sujet», *Gazette des Beaux-Arts*, mai—juin 1952, pp. 305—318, janvier 1953, pp. 27—36, décembre 1953, pp. 291—304, février 1954, pp. 67—76; Knuttel 1956, blz. 96; Левинсон-Лессинг 1956, с. VIII—IX; Виппер 1957, с. 312—314; Гос. Эрмитаж 1958, с. 252; А. Членов, «Кто героиня эрмитажной картины Рембрандта?», *Искусство*, 1960, № 6, с. 51—59; Levinson-Lessing 1964, Nos 72—75; Фехнер 1965, № 10; K. Clark, *Rembrandt and the Italian Renaissance*, London, 1966, pp. 108—110; Вольская 1966, с. 59—60; Егорова 1966, с. 93—94; Ю. И. Кузнецов, «Новое о картине Рембрандта *Даная*», *Сообщения Государственного Эрмитажа*, XXVII, 1966, с. 26—31; Bauch 1966, Nr 104; J. Kuznetzow, «Nieuws over Rembrandts *Danae*», *Oud-Holland*, LXXXlll, 1968, blz. 225—233; Gerson 1968, No 270; E. Brochhagen, «Beobachtungen an den Passionsbildern Rembrandts in München», *Festschrift Kauffmann. Minuscula discipulorum*, Berlin, 1968, S. 43; Haak 1968, blz. 138—139; Ch. Tümpel, «Studien zur Ikonographie der Historien Rembrandts», *Nederlands kunsthistorisch Jaarboek*, XX, 1969, blz. 158—160; Bredius, No 474; Ю. Кузнецов, *Загадки «Данаи». К истории создания картины Рембрандта*, Ленинград, 1970; Yu. Kuznetsov, "Rembrandt Discoveries at the Hermitage", *Apollo*, December 1974, pp. 488—490.

18. PORTRAIT OF AN OLD WOMAN

Oil on canvas. 82 × 72 cm
Signed and dated on the background, right: *Rembrandt f. 16(5)...*
The Pushkin Museum of Fine Arts, Moscow. No 2622

The loss of the last, and partially next to last, numerals of the date shows that a 4 cm wide strip of canvas was cut from the right-hand border. As a result, the correlation between the figure and surface has been disturbed; the original canvas was almost square in form, the empty space to the right of the figure being approximately the same as that on the left. The composition was more symmetrical than now. This distortion must be kept in mind when we evaluate the painter's original concept.
The portrait is of a rare quality. The outline of the shawl merges with the flowing silhouette of the velvet fur-trimmed cape. The bodice of the dark silk dress shimmers with different shades: obviously, such interplay was of high interest to the artist. Of startling beauty are the transparent folds of the white fabric and dark red shawl that frame the face. This picture is often

Portrait of an Old Woman. Face (X-ray photograph).
The Pushkin Museum of Fine Arts, Moscow

called *Portrait of an Old Woman in Sumptuous Dress,* in order to distinguish it from Rembrandt's other "old women". The feeling of controlled, refined luxury is the result of the master's rich technique; the dress itself is very much the same as on other women's portraits of that period. The only really extravagant touch is the sapphire ring — a little blue spark amidst the prevailing warm tones.

The dress has nothing in common with the Dutch fashion of the mid-seventeenth century. Imagined by the artist, it is reminiscent of the "Burgundy" dress. K. Bauch insists that the dark shawl, a favourite Rembrandt attribute often found in his paintings of old women, is a Hebrew "prayer shawl", and that in such portraits the model assumes the role of a biblical prophetess. Yet in the Moscow painting Rembrandt allowed himself no poetic "free play" when conveying the image and character of the model. The portrait is undoubtedly an excellent likeness. There is even a trace of formality, something that resembles his commissioned works, in the depiction of this intelligent, reticent, calm woman. In all probability the painter used the "Burgundy" costume simply because he found it attractive; he was not trying to hint at any biblical episode. A true and objective portrayal of the model is attained thanks to painstaking and masterly painting. The face is painted with layers of glaze, applied one over the other. The presence of thick white is minimal, as witnessed by the extremely "delicate", transparent X-ray plates. Until recently it was thought that the two last, and most important, digits of the date had been irreparably lost. Recent studies showed the remnants of the third digit near the cut-off border. It reads as 5. On the evidence of stylistic analysis the picture was previously dated between 1648 and 1650. Indeed, the painting of the face resembles Rembrandt's canvases of the 1640s. However, the majestic symmetry of the compositional scheme, as well as the brushwork of the dress, are characteristic of the following decade. Thus, the glazed black sleeves and the light ochre of the priming, evident on the bodice, are reminiscent of the dress in the 1654 *Portrait of an Old Woman* of the Pushkin Museum collection. The striking high impasto is apparent only on the white blouse and on the ring; the sapphire set in gold was first painted in white and then coated with a transparent blue dab.

Considering the psychological, compositional and technical peculiarities, one must probably date the painting between 1650 and 1652. The technique, now bold and sweeping, now precise and meticulous, the dignified and real-life quality of the model, make the *Portrait of an Old Woman* a most significant and interesting Rembrandt piece.

With the exception of the cut-off edge, the canvas is in excellent condition. There is slight retouching along the edges and on the woman's bodice.

PROVENANCE:

Until 1779   Robert Walpole Collection, Houghton Hall, England
     1779   Acquired for the Hermitage
     1930   The Pushkin Museum of Fine Arts, Moscow

EXHIBITIONS:

1936   Rembrandt. Moscow—Leningrad (Cat., pp. 45—46, No 17)
1956   Rembrandt and His School. Moscow—Leningrad (Cat., p. 56)
1969   Rembrandt. Moscow (Cat., pp. 13—14, 19)

LITERATURE:

Aedes Walpolianae, p. 48; Livret 1838, pp. 126—127, N° 28; Имп. Эрмитаж 1863—1916, № 823; Waagen 1864, S. 184; Bode 1883, S. 502—503; Bode—Hofstede de Groot 1897—1905, Nr 369; Valentiner 1909, S. 330, 560; Hofstede de Groot 1915, Nr 879, S. 364; Левинсон-Лессинг 1956, с. XV—XVI, табл. 18; Каталог ГМИИ 1961, с. 156; Виппер 1962, с. 351, 366; Фехнер 1965, № 18, с. 108—111; Егорова 1966, с. 72—73; Bauch 1966, Nr 277; Gerson 1968, pp. 389, 501, No 315; Bredius, No 371; Исследование картин Рембрандта, с. 400—402.

Old Man in an Armchair. 1652.
National Gallery, London

19. PORTRAIT OF AN OLD MAN IN RED

Oil on canvas, relined. 108 × 86 cm
The Hermitage, Leningrad. No 746

The 1650s witness a new flowering of Rembrandt's portraits. The number of commissioned portraits during that period is smaller, thus giving the painter greater freedom in his choice of model and interpretation. As in his youth, he turns to his closest acquaintances, his friends and relatives. His favourites are aged people who, in his opinion, provide the best material for psychological characterization, the main aim of the mature Rembrandt. His later portraits are distinguished by new and monumental forms. These are large portraits, half or three-quarter lengths; his models sit serenely in deep armchairs, usually facing the observer. The unknown old man in red of the Hermitage painting is depicted in much the same way.
The general impression is one of great inner strength and spiritual power, which explains why some scholars saw in this portrait the Greek sage Zeno. In all probability, we have here the portrait of a real person, whose great human dignity and nobility attracted the artist.
The expressive power is attained thanks to the most simple of devices, at least at first glance: the symmetrical placing of the figure, framed as it were by the oblong back of the chair, and the outwardly calm features of his face. This laconic style serves to enhance the feeling of grandiose monumentality of the portrait. The richness and versatility of Rembrandt's artistic language is revealed by the technique and the use of light. Colour is applied in broad, free strokes, thick in the lighted areas and thin, almost transparent in the shaded ones. Light, when falling on such a variegated surface, splits, and the figure appears to be surrounded by a vibrating medium of light and air.
The same old man is portrayed in a 1652 painting, the property of the National Gallery, London. The Hermitage portrait was done between 1652 and 1654. On the whole, the painting's condition is rather good. A 2.5 cm wide strip at the top and a 1.5 cm wide strip at the bottom were added later. The paint in the right upper corner was damaged, probably during restoration. Insignificant later overpaintings are discernible above the right shoulder and on the breast.

PROVENANCE:

Until 1769   Count Brühl Collection, Dresden
    1769   Acquired for the Hermitage

EXHIBITIONS:

1936   Rembrandt. Moscow—Leningrad (Cat., pp. 46—47, No 23)
1956   Rembrandt and His School. Moscow—Leningrad (Cat., p. 56)
1969—70   Rembrandt, His Precursors and Followers. Leningrad (Cat., p. 27, No 16)

LITERATURE:

Имп. Эрмитаж 1863—1916, № 818; Bode 1873, S. 10; Bode 1883, S. 503; J. Six, «De Homerus van Rembrandt», *Oud-Holland*, XVI, 1897, blz. 7—8; Valentiner 1909, S. 427; Hofstede de Groot 1915, Nr 440; Weisbach 1926, S. 548; Benesch 1935, S. 52; Rosenberg 1948, pp. 59—60; Hamann 1948, S. 392; Левинсон-Лессинг 1956, с. XV; Гос. Эрмитаж 1958, с. 256; Levinson-Lessing 1964, No 81; Фехнер 1965, № 19; Егорова 1966, с. 88—89; Bauch 1966, Nr 407; Gerson 1968, No 314; Bredius, No **274**.

Portrait of Adriaen van Rijn. 1650.
Mauritshuis Royal Picture Gallery,
The Hague

Portrait of Adriaen van Rijn.
1650—52. Louvre, Paris

Man with the Golden Helmet. *Ca.* 1650.
Dahlem Museum, Berlin

20. PORTRAIT OF ADRIAEN VAN RIJN, REMBRANDT'S BROTHER (?)

Oil on canvas, relined. 74 × 63 cm
Signed and dated on the background, left, above the shoulder: *Rembrandt f. 1654*
The Pushkin Museum of Fine Arts, Moscow. No 2627

The man on the portrait was probably among Rembrandt's constant associates. We find him
in three other portraits: at The Hague (1650), in Paris (*ca.* 1650—52) and in the Berlin *Man
with the Golden Helmet* (*ca.* 1650). Toward the end of the last century a theory was advanced
stating that the painter's older brother Adriaen van Rijn was the model for all four portraits.
According to the scanty data available, he lived all his life in Leyden where he was a shoemak-
er; in 1639 he inherited his father's windmill, and died in 1651 or 1652.
The above-mentioned theory was accepted in scientific literature with certain reservations. The
most serious argument against it was the date of the Moscow painting, 1654, since Adriaen
van Rijn was known to have died no later than 1652. Seeking to reconcile these facts, another
theory was suggested according to which Rembrandt created this picture after his brother's

Portrait of Adriaen van Rijn, Rembrandt's Brother (?).
Face (X-ray photograph). The Pushkin Museum of Fine Arts, Moscow

Portrait of Adriaen van Rijn, Rembrandt's Brother (?)
(infra-red photograph). The Pushkin Museum of Fine Arts, Moscow

death. But such practice is an exception to the rule where Rembrandt is concerned. Moreover, the attempt to convey a concrete emotional state and concrete surrounding conditions is so obvious in the Moscow painting as to undermine any such theory.

In most paintings of those years we find a thoroughly thought-out artistic system. It is evident, for instance, in *Portrait of an Old Woman* (1654), now in the Pushkin Museum, Moscow. Quite to the contrary, *Portrait of Adriaen van Rijn* is distinguished by a singular spontaneity. Succumbing to visual and emotional impressions, the painter follows the interplay of soft reflections of light on the old man's thoughtful face, enveloped, as it were, in glimmering shadow. The features are built by short, freely applied brush-strokes of different shades.

Perhaps the model's dominating influence brought about an unsatisfactory result. At any rate, the painter made certain changes, all of them pertaining to less important details. In the first version, a thick strip of white travelled the length of the collar; later it was covered by black glaze. The relief of white, discernible on the picture's surface, and the continuous downward strokes of white are especially evident in X-rays. Quite possibly, the old sitter was dressed in a white shirt. When transferred to canvas, this white patch stood out too sharply against the subdued tone of the background and contrasted with the soft chiaroscuro of the face. Rembrandt hastened to black it out, and while doing so extended the black area downward, thus adding another vertical constructive element supporting the composition. The correction was done when the underlying coat of paint had not yet dried, which resulted in the subsequent appearance of craquelures in the black glaze.

At the same time, Rembrandt added some other changes. Drawing a long black line on the dried brown surface of the old man's coat, he traced the seam on the right shoulder. Of special importance to the composition are the changes in the silhouette of the beret, quite apparent in infra-red photography. In the first version, it rose higher above the head and descended lower to the left of the neck, the general outline being rounder. Rembrandt partially covered it with the light ochre of the background, and probably moved it somewhat further to the right. The black silhouette of the beret became horizontally elongated, balancing the black vertical that appeared below. All the changes pursue one aim — to strengthen the constructive element of the composition and arrive at a balanced correlation between the old man's face and the surrounding painting. These changes help create a special, intensely individual, spiritual atmosphere.

The suggestion that this painting is a pair with the 1654 Moscow *Portrait of an Old Woman* (see No 23) cannot be accepted.

The painting is covered with a thick coat of old varnish. There is overpainting on the hand and lower edge of the canvas. A small loss of paint is apparent near the collar.

PROVENANCE:

1760	Count Brühl Collection, Dresden
1769	Acquired for the Hermitage
1930	The Pushkin Museum of Fine Arts, Moscow

EXHIBITIONS:

1936   Rembrandt. Moscow—Leningrad (Cat., p. 46, No 19)
1956   Rembrandt and His School. Moscow—Leningrad (Cat., pp. 56—57)
1969   Rembrandt. Moscow (Cat., pp. 14, 16, 18)

LITERATURE:

Catalogue 1774, N° 88; Livret 1838, p. 127, N° 29; Имп. Эрмитаж 1863—1916, № 824; Waagen 1864, S. 183; Bode—Hofstede de Groot 1897—1905, Nr 360; F. Laban, «Rembrandts Bildnis seines Bruders Adriaen Harmensz van Rijn in der Berliner Galerie», *Zeitschrift für bildende Kunst*, IX, 1897—1898, S. 75—78; Valentiner 1909, S. 421; Hofstede de Groot 1915, S. 201, Nr 442; Benesch 1935, S. 46, 52; Левинсон-Лессинг 1956, с. XV—XVI, табл. 20; Knuttel 1956, blz. 172; Bauch 1960, S. 169—170; Каталог ГМИИ 1961, с. 156; Виппер 1962, с. 394, 407; I. Antonova (introd.), *Le Musée de Moscou*, Paris, 1963, pp. 116—117; Фехнер 1965, № 23, с. 130—132; Егорова 1966, с. 79—81; Альбом ГМИИ 1966, № 33; Bauch 1966, Nr 406; Gerson 1968, pp. 18, 382, 500, No 302; Bredius, No 131; К. Егорова, *Портрет в творчестве Рембрандта*, Москва, 1975, с. 126—127; Исследование картин Рембрандта, с. 403—407.

An Old Woman Reading. 1655.
The Duke of Buccleuch Collection,
Scotland

21. PORTRAIT OF AN OLD WOMAN

Oil on canvas, relined. 109 × 84.5 cm (enlarged on the sides and at the bottom), originally
89 × 76.5 cm
Signed and dated at bottom, left: *Rembrandt f. 1654.*
The Hermitage, Leningrad. No 738

Certain scholars believe this to be the portrait of Rembrandt's sister-in-law Elisabeth van Leeuwen.
The reasons for this identification were that another portrait depicting this woman (Pushkin
Museum of Fine Arts, Moscow, Bredius 383, see No 23) is considered to be the pendant to
the same museum's portrait, supposedly of Rembrandt's brother (Bredius 131, see No 20). At
the present date, the Moscow canvases are not considered to be companion portraits. The Hermitage portrait in question is probably pendant to *Portrait of an Old Jew*, also of the Hermitage collection (Bredius 270, see No 22).
Be that as it may, the Hermitage old woman (also to be found, besides Moscow, in the Duke
of Buccleuch collection in Scotland, Bredius 385) was one of the painter's close acquaintances.

Portrait of an Old Woman. Face (X-ray photograph).
The Hermitage, Leningrad

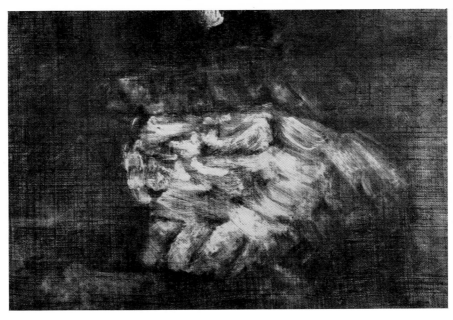

Portrait of an Old Woman. Hands (X-ray photograph).
The Hermitage, Leningrad

Portrait of an Old Woman, and similar works, belong to the type called "biography portraits" in art literature. They do not fix a given moment, but aim to convey a continuous flow of emotions and tell something of the model's past and present. Indeed, the old woman's face and her callous hands so wearily folded on her lap, are like a book telling the long and sad story of her life. Her eyes that look not at but through the observer, into space, arouse a wish to know her life story and inner world, for it is the gaze of a person steeped in thought and memories. One's eyes are drawn to her face, softly lit up by the white kerchief on her breast — the only bright spot in her sombre-coloured apparel. The old woman of the Hermitage painting is one of Rembrandt's most attractive women's portrayals. Her image seems to breathe forth goodness and gentleness.
The painting is in good condition. Later additions at the bottom and on the sides have been removed. Overpaintings are apparent on the background, on the arm of the chair and on the woman's hands.

PROVENANCE:

Until 1781   Baudouin Collection, Paris
      1781   Acquired for the Hermitage

EXHIBITIONS:

1936   Rembrandt. Moscow—Leningrad (Cat., p. 46, No 21)
1956   Rembrandt. Amsterdam—Rotterdam (Cat. No 67)
1968   Masterpieces of Rembrandt. Tokyo—Kioto (Cat. No 9)
1969—70   Rembrandt, His Precursors and Followers. Leningrad (Cat., p. 28, No 19)

LITERATURE:

Имп. Эрмитаж 1863—1916, № 805; Bode 1873, S. 10; Bode 1883, S. 502, 600; Valentiner 1909, S. 423; Hofstede de Groot 1915, Nr 506; Weisbach 1926, S. 551; Benesch 1935, S. 52; Rosenberg 1948, p. 59; Hamann 1948, S. 183, 186; Левинсон-Лессинг 1956, с. XV; Гос. Эрмитаж 1958, с. 259; Виппер 1962, с. 397, 407; Фехнер 1965, № 22; Егорова 1966, с. 85—86; Bauch 1966, Nr 274; Gerson 1968, No 312; Bredius, No 381.

22. PORTRAIT OF AN OLD JEW

Oil on canvas, relined. 109 × 84.8 cm (enlarged on both sides and at the bottom), originally 89 × 76.5 cm
Signed and dated on the background, left, near the shoulder: *Rembrandt. f. 1654*
The Hermitage, Leningrad. No 737

Holland was a religiously tolerant country. Many Jews fled there from Spain and Portugal, escaping the all-powerful Inquisition. The majority of the Jewish community of Amsterdam lived in the Jodenbreestraat, thus being next-door neighbours of Rembrandt. It was in this environment that Rembrandt, a man who was well versed in the Bible, found the models for his biblical and evangelic compositions. We come across them in his etchings and canvases. We know some of them by name, while the names of many others remain unknown, as, for instance, that of the old man whose wise and expressive face looks at us from the Hermitage painting. The man's strange attire, the robe-like dress and large, flat beret of black velvet, make it quite clear that this was no run-of-the-mill commissioned portrait. As in the *Old Man in Red*, the

Portrait of an Old Jew. Face (X-ray photograph).
The Hermitage, Leningrad

Portrait of an Old Jew. Hands (X-ray photograph).
The Hermitage, Leningrad

architectonic composition (here in the shape of a triangle, its wide base being the armchair's elbow-supports) lends a monumental aspect to the model. The solemn and sombre combination of red, brown and black is in complete harmony with the severe face, uncommonly powerful in its expressiveness and strength.

The painting is possibly a pendant to *Portrait of an Old Woman* (see No 21), but the conclusion that the models are man and wife does not necessarily follow. To begin with, the man's face is turned to the right, not left; secondly, we have the example of Gerard Dou, who unites in his companion portraits of the Cassel Picture Gallery Rembrandt's mother and an old man who probably was never her husband. The problem of uncommissioned pair portraits in Rembrandt's late period still presents difficulties. Pair portraits of parents or grandparents decorating the walls of burgher homes acquired the same role in Dutch everyday life of the second half of the seventeenth century as portrait galleries of ancestors in the castles of aristocrats. Perhaps his family's origin was less important to the Dutch burgher than its wealth and famous deeds. But it would seem as though Rembrandt's "old men" and "old women" represent a special theme, which might be qualified in a general way as "old people" or "ancestors". Yet in his "old people" the painter seeks to portray, above all, their wisdom and experience, rather than their noble origin, wealth or business acumen.

The canvas is in good condition. Later additions at the bottom and on the sides have been removed. Apart from overpaintings on the background there is a restored break in the area of the right wrist.

PROVENANCE:

Until 1781   Baudouin Collection, Paris
      1781   Acquired for the Hermitage

EXHIBITIONS:

1936   Rembrandt. Moscow—Leningrad (Cat., p. 46, No 22)
1956   Rembrandt and His School. Moscow — Leningrad (Cat., p. 57)
1968   Masterpieces of Rembrandt. Tokyo—Kioto (Cat. No 8)
1969—70 Rembrandt, His Precursors and Followers. Leningrad (Cat., p. 28, No 18)

LITERATURE:

Имп. Эрмитаж 1863—1916, № 810; Bode 1873, S. 10; Bode 1883, S. 503; Valentiner 1909, S. 427; Hofstede de Groot 1915, Nr 439; Weisbach 1926, S. 550; Benesch 1935, S. 52; Rosenberg 1948, p. 59; Hamann 1948, S. 392; Левинсон-Лессинг 1958, с. 259; Фехнер 1965, № 21; Егорова 1966, с. 85—86; Bauch 1966, Nr 210; Gerson 1968, No 313; Bredius, No 270.

23. PORTRAIT OF AN OLD WOMAN

Oil on canvas, relined. 74 × 63 cm
Signed and dated on the background, left, above the shoulder: *Rembrandt f. 1654.*
The Pushkin Museum of Fine Arts, Moscow. No 2624

The canvas has the same dimensions and is dated the same year as *Portrait of Adriaen van Rijn* (see No 20); both pictures come from the Dresden collection of Count Brühl where they probably constituted a symmetrical pair, as was the vogue in the eighteenth century. Suggestions to this effect may be found in early Hermitage inventories and catalogues, but serious authors of that museum's nineteenth century catalogues refrain from such suppositions. In the early twentieth century W. R. Valentiner revived the idea in his reference book on Rembrandt; with some reservations, he drew definite conclusions concerning the identity of the model. He had no doubts that the man was Adriaen van Rijn; hence the second portrait of the pair must be his wife, Rembrandt's sister-in-law. As a result, the lengthy German title, *Portrait of the Wife of Rembrandt's Brother*, made its way into catalogues and remained there for many years.

Portrait of an Old Woman. Face (X-ray photograph).
The Pushkin Museum of Fine Arts, Moscow

Yet these two pictures differ from one another as greatly as is only possible for the works of the same genre, painted by the same author and at the same time. They differ deeply in colour scheme, in composition (the figures are differently correlated with the surrounding space and the canvas surface), and in mood. They are painted in a different emotional key. This is especially evident when the two portraits hang side by side. It is noteworthy that the author of the 1893 Hermitage catalogue, A. Somov, had one more serious reason to doubt the pair theory. Somov discovered that the same woman figures in another Hermitage portrait, which also has its companion portrait of a man (see Nos 21 and 22). What is more, the bond between the latter two paintings is much more convincing. Thus it may be said that the two Moscow portraits of 1654 were not conceived as companion portraits by the artist: this was the doing of one of their owners. The identification of the woman as Rembrandt's sister-in-law has been refuted, along with the still more fantastic supposition that the picture portrays the painter's mother. The latter can be found in inventories and catalogues of the eighteenth and early nineteenth centuries, when biographical data concerning Rembrandt and his family were scarce. Whoever this woman was, she led the painter to produce one of his masterpieces. Rembrandt's concept of man and his fate is most profoundly expressed in this portrait.

The picture is an example of perfect balance and precision. The painting of the face gives an impression of high impasto, while in reality this is not the case. The impression is due to a contrast with the supremely delicate glazing of the accessories. Here and there, on the breast and sleeves, sandy patches of ochre-tinged priming show through the black dabs. Combined with the long, thin strokes of black and white, these yellowish spots create a complex interplay of pleats on the front of the woman's dress. X-ray plates are almost completely transparent, excepting the central part of the painting. Here most prominent are the strokes of white lead used in the painting of the face and white scarf.

It is often believed that expressive, clear-cut strokes are possible only when the artist utilizes a thick mixture of paints, based on white. Rembrandt's work disproves this view. He applies liquid, transparent, dark glaze, using a most varied technique. The stabbing strokes of his hard brush create a moving, lifelike quality of the background; long, broad strokes convey the deep velvety black of the sleeves; narrow, delicate touches with the tip of a soft brush are applied for the pleats of the thin fabric on the breast, etc.

Rembrandt liked to apply a few bold strokes over a thin layer of paint, thus emphasizing the relief, colour and form. Thus, the elongated strokes of red overrunning the seemingly dusted with ashes reddish spot, set off the outline of the shawl, while dark underlying shadows separate it from the face. Traces of white on the X-ray plate show that in the first version a white fabric hung from under the dark red shawl along either side of the face; later, the painter blacked it out. This certainly served to enhance the mood of tragic meditation that dominated the old woman's aspect.

The variegated technique is especially evident thanks to the excellent condition of the painting. Minor overpaintings are present only in the border areas of the canvas. In the central part a bit of shading, of very old date, is applied to the woman's forehead.

PROVENANCE:

1760	Count Brühl Collection, Dresden
1769	Acquired for the Hermitage
1930	The Pushkin Museum of Fine Arts, Moscow

EXHIBITIONS:

1936	Rembrandt. Moscow—Leningrad (Cat., p. 46, No 20)
1956	Rembrandt and His School. Moscow—Leningrad (Cat., p. 57)
1969	Rembrandt. Moscow (Cat., pp. 10—11, 16, 21)

LITERATURE:

Catalogue 1774, N° 97; Livret 1838, p. 121, N° 6; Имп. Эрмитаж 1863—1916, № 806; Waagen 1864, S. 183; Bode 1873, S. 10; Bode—Hofstede de Groot 1897—1905, Nr 394; Valentiner 1909, S. 421; Hofstede de Groot 1915, S. 223—224, Nr 507; Weisbach 1926, S. 551; Benesch 1935, S. 52; Лазарев 1936, с. 37; Левинсон-Лессинг 1956, с. XV—XVI, табл. 21; Ротенберг 1956, с. 36; Каталог ГМИИ 1961, с. 156; Виппер 1962, с. 395, 407—408; I. Antonova (introd.), *Le Musée de Moscou*, Paris, 1963, pp. 118—119; Фехнер 1965, № 24, с. 133—135; Егорова 1966, с. 87—88; Альбом ГМИИ 1966, № 34; Bauch 1966, Nr 275; Gerson 1968, pp. 382, 501, No 303; Bredius, No 383.

Saskia (?) before the Mirror. 1630s. Drawing.
Ancient Art Museum, Brussels

24. YOUNG WOMAN WITH EARRINGS

Oil on oak, cradled. 39.5 × 32.5 cm. Upper corners enlarged by later additions: left, a triangle with sides measuring 9.7 × 4.5 cm; right, another measuring 9.5 × 4.3 cm. Added later to the lower border, a strip 7.2 cm wide.
Signed and dated left, on the casket: *Rembrandt. f. 1657*
The Hermitage, Leningrad. No 784

The sitter in this picture was probably Hendrickje Stoffels. This supposition is corroborated not so much by portrait likeness as by the painter's attitude towards his model. The picture gives the impression of having been done in one glorious surge: the warm, golden tone, the hot reds, yellows and pinks, the passionate brush-strokes, caressing and delicate when the artist paints the face, or quick and energetic when he paints outlying areas. However, X-ray investigation shows the final position of the fingers of the right hand to have been found only after some time. The motif so brilliantly executed here was the result of long meditation, as testified to by drawings. Moreover, its solution was partially anticipated in Rembrandt's drawing *Saskia (?) before a Mirror* at the Ancient Art Museum in Brussels (Benesch A 7). Fritz Saxl even believed this drawing to be a preparatory stage for the final painting, and dated it 1654 (the date of the Hermitage painting had been erroneously read as 1654, instead of 1657). The majority of scholars, however, date the drawing much earlier — about 1635 (W. R. Valentiner, L. van Puyvelde, O. Benesch).
Hofstede de Groot suggested that the Hermitage painting was the author's partial copy of the portrait of Rembrandt and Saskia from the Buckingham Palace collection in London. This idea has long been rejected, and the Buckingham Palace painting recognized as the work of some pupil of Rembrandt, for whom the *Young Woman with Earrings* served as a study.
W. Martin voiced the possibility of our picture being only a fragment. G. Gluck refuted this and identified the Hermitage painting as the one entered in the 1656 inventory of Rembrandt's estate under No 39 and called *Courtesan Combing Her Hair*. Besides the fact that this title hardly seems to fit the scene portrayed in the *Young Woman with Earrings*, Gluck's suggestion must be rejected on other grounds: a painting dated 1657 could not possibly figure in the inventory of 1656.
The original form of the panel was octagonal. Evidently the upper corners were added at a later stage, after the lower part of the picture was lost and then reconstructed, minus the cut-off corners.
Overpainting is applied over the joints with later additions, partly covering the original painting. On the whole the painting is in good condition.

PROVENANCE:

1717	Coonrad Droste Collection, The Hague
1734	July 21: sold for 50 florins at the auction of the Coonrad Droste Collection
1748	April 22: on sale at the auction of the Godefroy Collection in Paris, bought by Agard
Until 1781	Baudouin Collection, Paris
1781	Acquired for the Hermitage

EXHIBITIONS:

1936   Rembrandt. Moscow—Leningrad (Cat., p. 46, No 24)

1956   Rembrandt and His School. Moscow—Leningrad (Cat., p. 58)

1969—70   Rembrandt, His Precursors and Followers. Leningrad (Cat., p. 27, No 17)

LITERATURE:

Имп. Эрмитаж 1863—1916, № 817; Bode 1883, S. 504, 602; A. Bredius, «Kritische Bemerkungen zur Amsterdamer Rembrandt-Ausstellung», *Zeitschrift für bildende Kunst*, II, 1898/99, S. 168; F. Saxl, *Repertorium für Kunstwissenschaft*, 1908, S. 344; Valentiner 1909, S. 405; Hofstede de Groot 1915, Nr 309; C. Hofstede de Groot, *Die holländische Kritik der jetzigen Rembrandt-Forschung und neuest gefundene Rembrandtsbilder*, Stuttgart—Berlin, 1922, S. 18; Benesch 1935, S. 52; Hamann 1948, S. 95—97; Левинсон-Лессинг, 1956, с. XVI—XVII; Гос. Эрмитаж 1958, с. 259; Фехнер 1955, № 20; Bauch 1966, Nr 272; Gerson 1968, No 279; Bredius, No 387.

Christ and the Woman of Samaria. 1658. Etching

25. CHRIST AND THE WOMAN OF SAMARIA

Oil on canvas, relined. 60 × 75 cm
Signed and dated on the well: *Rembrandt f. 1659* (the signature is authentic, though restored at a later date)
The Hermitage, Leningrad. No 714

The picture treats an evangelic subject, and shows Christ revealing himself to the woman of Samaria (*John*, 4. 4—27).

The Hermitage composition is the final and most significant of a series of paintings on a theme that attracted Rembrandt in the 1650s. Besides the Hermitage painting, two more are known to have been produced on the same subject during this period, both dated 1655 (Dahlem Museum, Berlin, and Metropolitan Museum of Art, New York, Bredius 588, 589), as well as several drawings and one etching (1658, Bartsch 70). *Christ and the Woman of Samaria* was long ignored by scholars. An eighteenth century Hermitage acquisition, the painting soon went to the private apartments of the Yekaterininsky Palace in Tsarskoye Selo, where it was discovered only in 1898 by A. Somov, director of the picture gallery, who returned it to the Hermitage and had it restored. It was then that the signature and date were brought to light.

The poor state of preservation led some scholars, who had no opportunity to see the painting, to question its authenticity. The same makes a complete estimation of its original artistic worth impossible. But even in its present state, the Hermitage canvas demonstrates the artist's urge to achieve a Renaissance-like architectonic clarity and a mood of high spirituality, — features that find their most poetical expression in the works of the Venetian school, and are so apparent in Rembrandt's creations of the late 1650s. The semicircular arcades of the well frame both of the speakers, turned toward each other in such a fashion as to make the composition seem a diptych, while the broad frontal arch underlines their bi-entity. In the right third of the painting, the compact group of disciples, standing on the level of the well's wall, and the lonely building, towering on the summit of a hill, match each of the two other thirds of the composition, which is highlighted by the woman's bright pink-and-white apparel. These characteristics appear in the 1658 etching of the same name, but it is in the Hermitage painting that they find their fullest embodiment.

It is hard to say what moment of the dialogue, half a chapter long in the Gospel, is depicted here. Comparison with the painting of the William Timken collection in New York (1655), in which Christ's gesture toward the building on the hill is more obvious and which, therefore, is considered to illustrate his words, "Woman, believe me, the hour cometh, when ye shall neither in this mountain, nor yet at Jerusalem, worship the Father," permits us to assume that the Hermitage painting represents the same moment.

The painting had seriously suffered in the eighteenth century and since then was subject to multiple restorations. The upper layer of paint is washed out in many places. There are numerous later overpaintings both on the figures and on the sky and the well.

PROVENANCE:

1741	April 12: on sale at the auction of the Bicker van Zweiten Collection, The Hague (6 florins)
Ca. 1780—91	Potemkin Collection
1792	Acquired for the Hermitage

Until 1898   Part of the Yekaterininsky Palace Collection in Tsarskoye Selo
1898   Returned to the Hermitage

EXHIBITIONS:

1956   Rembrandt and His School. Moscow—Leningrad (Cat., p. 59)
1968—69   The Age of Rembrandt. Tokyo—Kioto (Cat. No 49)
1969—70   Rembrandt, His Precursors and Followers. Leningrad (Cat., p. 28, No 20)

LITERATURE:

Hoet 1752, II, blz. 12; Имп. Эрмитаж 1863—1916, № 1858; A. de Somof, «Les nouveaux Rembrandt et Adam Elsheimer à l'Ermitage Impérial», *Gazette des Beaux-Arts*, 21, 1899, pp. 260—262; Valentiner 1909, S. 389; Hofstede de Groot 1915, Nr 102; Weisbach 1926, S. 422, 460; Hamann 1948, S. 382—383; Гос. Эрмитаж 1958, с. 264; Фехнер 1965, № 25; Bauch 1966, Nr 91; Gerson 1968, No 349; Bredius, No 592 A.

Emperor Jahangir Receiving an
Address. 1650s. Drawing.
British Museum, London

26. AHASUERUS, HAMAN AND ESTHER

Oil on canvas, relined. 73 × 94 cm
Signed and dated in the lower left corner: *Rembrandt f. 1660*
The Pushkin Museum of Fine Arts, Moscow. No 297

Haman, the all-powerful minister of King Ahasuerus's Babylonian court, falsely accused the
Jewish subjects of wicked thoughts and insubordinance, and a day was fixed when all Jews
were to be exterminated. Esther, wife of King Ahasuerus, invited Haman and the King to a
banquet she had prepared, and there asked the King to spare herself and her people. "And
Esther said, The adversary and enemy is this wicked Haman. Then Haman was afraid before the
king and the queen" (*Esther*, 7. 6). This dramatic biblical episode was very popular in seventeenth century painting. Artists usually depicted the sumptuous setting of the feast, the King's
surprise and anger, Esther's triumph and Haman's fear. This interpretation was typical: it applied
as well to Rembrandt's painting. In 1662, two years after its creation, a book of poems by
the well-known playwright and poet Jan Voss was published. Several of his verses have the
common title: "Certain Pictures in the House of the Honourable Jan Jakobsen Hinlopen, Syndic

Ahasuerus, Haman and Esther. Detail (infra-red photograph).
The Pushkin Museum of Fine Arts, Moscow

Ahasuerus, Haman and Esther (ultraviolet photograph).
The Pushkin Museum of Fine Arts, Moscow

of Amsterdam". Here is a prosaic translation of one of them: "*Haman invited by Esther and Ahasuerus, painted by Rembrandt.* Here one sees Haman feasting with Ahasuerus and Esther. But all is in vain, his breast nearly bursts with vexation and grief, he tastes of Esther's delicacies, but even deeper buries his teeth in her heart. The furious King seeks vengeance..." It is indeed difficult to relate such a histrionic description to the meditating protagonists of Rembrandt's picture.

Esther and Haman are inclined slightly forward in a pose that signifies obedience to fate and the King. Their eyes follow that movement. Ignoring each other, they look downward. Their struggle is completely void of outward dramatism, it is transferred to the realm of the spiritual, the ethical. The King, steeped in meditation, looks straight ahead. It seems as though he is preoccupied not so much with the fates of Haman and Esther as with the problem of good and evil in the world, veracity and perfidy of human nature. Instead of merely illustrating the biblical episode, Rembrandt creates a picture revealing the spiritual essence of man's life.

Esther's expressive gesture emphasizes what she has just said: disclosing the truth to the King, she gives herself and her people into his hands. The King clasps his sceptre: its touch means life to the righteous. The sunken, trembling Haman automatically grasps his goblet. The poses and gestures of all three speak as eloquently as their faces.

The banquet is more hinted at than actually represented — there are only a plate with two apples, Haman's goblet and the Oriental pitcher near the table. A wealth of still life, though called for by the subject-matter, would actually be out of place here. The protagonists are seated around the table on cushions, for such was the fashion, as the painter believed, of not only the modern, but the ancient Orient, too. In the 1650s Rembrandt had at his disposal a book of Indian miniatures; he made sketches from it that delicately conveyed the artistic peculiarities of the original. The dress and pose of Haman, for instance, are quite similar to those of the *Emperor Jahangir Receiving an Address* (British Museum, Benesch 1190). Much to the contrary, the apparel of Ahasuerus, and especially of Esther, is clearly the product of the artist's imagination. Here, as in his reading of the biblical text, he refuses to be tied down by facts; he only leans on them, while following the laws of his own creative thought.

According to Rembrandt's concept, the visual effect of the picture depended on the correlation between the lighted central area and the surrounding space. Today this effect is rarely observed, as it calls for exceptionally strong light. It is only then that the vigorous brush-strokes of the red-brown glaze become apparent in the lower part of the picture and in the background around Haman. His figure, almost completely structured on glazing, merges with the shimmering surrounding area. In contrast, the King's dazzling apparel stands out against the black background of the hanging curtain. The figure of Esther is the dominating element thanks to the intense and precise colouring and the expressive surface texture. Her brocade robe, jewels and crown are painted in impasto strokes, the interplay of which is stressed by the neighbouring dark glaze background.

Infra-red photography shows long dark lines that partially coincide with the black strokes tracing some of the objects in the lower part of the picture. When completing a painting, Rembrandt often used this technique to emphasize the contour of this or that object. However, some of the lines, apparent on the film, do not merge with the silhouette and at times are covered by a layer of lighter colour. One of these traces, though not exactly, Ahasuerus's turban, while another serves as the vertical axis of his figure. Shorter and less distinct lines can be seen behind the heads of Haman and Esther, along the table's surface, etc. They probably belong to the first compositional sketch of the painting. Rembrandt traced the basic outlines and sections of the picture in quick strokes of black. Later they were covered with layers of paint, but in certain places are apparent in infra-red photography.

The painting is of a kind that, seemingly, should easily have stood up to the wear and tear of time. All or almost all of the picture's owners, during the century-long period prior to its acquisition in 1764 for the Hermitage collection, are known to us. One of them bears the blame for the heavy damage inflicted on the picture. In an inventory dated 1773 the damaged condition is already mentioned. According to data supplied by the Hermitage archives, the restorer A. Mitrokhin transferred the painting from the old canvas to a new one in 1819. White lead was used for the new priming, which made subsequent X-ray study extremely difficult. The canvas had to be relined as early as 1829. The painting was once more transferred to a new canvas in 1900 by the restorer Hauser in Berlin, and again *ca.* 1924—26 in the restoration shops of the Pushkin Museum of Fine Arts. By 1970 the surface showed numerous blisters combined with deep craquelures. Close study reveals numerous overpaintings, both old (on Ahasuerus's face and Esther's arm) and comparatively recent. Traces of serious repainting are apparent on the left part of Ahasuerus's turban. To prevent possible losses of paint, another transfer of the painting to a new canvas has been successfully carried out in 1974 by S. Churakov, the leading restorer of the Museum.

Naturally, the poor condition of the painting makes any full evaluation of the artist's work hazardous, yet the picture is certainly one of Rembrandt's outstanding creations.

Evidently Rembrandt turned to the story of Esther several times. The large canvas entitled *Mordecai before Esther and Ahasuerus* in Bucharest is usually attributed to one of Rembrandt's pupils, but there is every reason to believe that this work reflects the teacher's concept. This assumption is corroborated by an undoubtedly authentic compositional sketch belonging to the Pushkin Museum of Fine Arts, — the unknown to Benesch reverse side of the drawing *Rembrandt's Kitchen* (Benesch 747). On the other hand, the authenticity of the drawing from the Netherlandish Institute in Paris (the Fritz Lugt collection, earlier in the Prince Lichtenstein collection) is questionable, although it partly repeats the Moscow painting's composition (Hofstede de Groot 1503, not mentioned by Benesch). Specialists are uncertain about the attribution of a strikingly expressive drawing from Budapest which depicts the next stage in the biblical episode, i.e. that of Ahasuerus's wrath (Benesch 1067).

PROVENANCE:

1662	J. Hinlopen Collection, Amsterdam; later, Geelvink Collection
1760	Sold at The Hague with the G. Hoet Collection
Until 1764	Gotzkowsky Collection, Berlin
1764	Acquired for the Hermitage
1862	Rumiantsev Museum, Moscow
1924	The Pushkin Museum of Fine Arts, Moscow

EXHIBITIONS:

1936	Rembrandt. Moscow—Leningrad (Cat., p. 47, No 25)
1956	Rembrandt and His School. Moscow—Leningrad (Cat., pp. 59—60)
1969	Rembrandt. Moscow (Cat., p. 20)

LITERATURE:

Terwesten 1770, p. 225, Nr 45; Catalogue 1774, N° 82; *Каталог картин Московского Публичного Музеума*, Москва, 1862, с. 9, № 78; Bode—Hofstede de Groot 1897—1905, Nr 411; C. Hofstede de Groot, *Urkunden über Rembrandt*, Den Haag, 1906, Nr 247, 407; Valentiner 1909, S. 453; П. В., «*Агасфер и Аман у Эсфири*. Румянцевский музей, Москва», *Старые годы*, 1910, февраль, с. 41—42; Hofstede de Groot 1915, S. 30—31, Nr 46; *Императорский Московский Публичный и Румянцевский музей. Каталог картинной галереи*, Москва, 1915, с. 250—251, 270 (plate facing p. 202); Bredius 1937, p. 530; Hamann 1948, S. 410—411, 413; Rosenberg 1948, p. 22; Левинсон-Лессинг 1956, с. XVIII—XIX, табл. 25; Ротенберг 1956, с. 33—35; И. Линник, «К вопросу о сюжете картины Рембрандта из собрания Эрмитажа», *Искусство*, 1956, № 7, с. 46—47; В. Н. Вольская, «Рембрандт среди своих современников», *Искусство*, 1956, № 7, с. 40; Knuttel 1956, pp. 208—209; Каталог ГМИИ 1961, с. 156; Виппер 1962, с. 433, 437; J. G. van Gelder e. a., *Fritz Lugt. Zijn leven en zijn verzamelingen*, 's-Gravenhage, 1964, blz. 25; J. Gantner, *Rembrandt und die Verwandlung klassischer Formen*, Bern—München, 1964, S. 162—164; Фехнер 1965, с. 138—141, № 26; Bauch 1966, Nr 37; Альбом ГМИИ 1966, № 32; Gerson 1968, pp. 416, 502, No 351; Bredius, No 530; Исследование картин Рембрандта, с. 410—413; К. С. Егорова, *Картина Рембрандта «Артаксеркс, Аман и Эсфирь» и ее реставрация*, Москва, 1975.

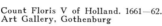

Count Floris V of Holland. 1661—62.
Art Gallery, Gothenburg

Man with a Gold Chain. 1657.
California Palace of the Legion of
Honour, San Francisco

27. PORTRAIT OF A MAN

Oil on canvas, relined. 71 × 61 cm
Signed and dated near the shoulder, left: *Rembrandt. f. 1661.*
The Hermitage, Leningrad. No 751

The portraits of the 1660s assume a quality of unparalleled grandeur stemming from the painter's deep penetration into man's inner world. It is in this calm state of concentrated meditation that we see the unknown bearded man on the portrait of 1661.

This face is not new to Rembrandt's work. Especially noteworthy is the portrait in the London National Gallery which, according to specialists, is one of Rembrandt's most expressive. We see the same man as Aristotle in the famous *Aristotle Contemplating the Bust of Homer* (Metropolitan Museum of Art, New York, Bredius 478). Since this painting is dated 1653, while the Hermitage picture was produced in 1661, one may assume that this man was one of Rembrandt's friends, and of long standing at that. Perhaps the spiritual qualities that such a strangely serious and melancholy man must have possessed tempted Rembrandt to paint him as an ancient Greek philosopher.

The same man was probably the model for the *Count Floris V of Holland* (Art Gallery, Gothenburg) and the *Man with a Gold Chain* (1657, California Palace of the Legion of Honour, San Francisco). The handsome, noble countenance of the man in the Hermitage painting gave Rembrandt reason to choose him as a model for significant historical personages. It is quite possible, therefore, that the Hermitage painting is not simply a portrait *per se*, but the fantasy portrait of a historical personage, as testified to by the rich and extravagant dress, and the grand pose. The deep characterization and the supreme quality of the brushwork, especially apparent after the recently performed regeneration of the dimmed varnish, establish this painting as one of the Hermitage collection's prize works.

The picture is in good condition. Besides some slight overpaintings on the background and the dress, there is a small loss of paint and priming on the left-eye pupil. This loss, painted over in a lighter tone, resembles a tear, thus accentuating the somewhat melancholy expression of the man's face.

PROVENANCE:

Until 1829   Collection of the Duchess of Saint-Leu, Paris
       1829   Acquired for the Hermitage

EXHIBITIONS:

1936   Rembrandt. Moscow—Leningrad (Cat., p. 47, No 26)
1956   Rembrandt and His School. Moscow—Leningrad (Cat., p. 60)
1968—69   The Age of Rembrandt. Tokyo—Kioto (Cat. No 50)
1969—70   Rembrandt, His Precursors and Followers. Leningrad (Cat., p. 29, No 21)

LITERATURE:

Имп. Эрмитаж 1863—1916, № 821; Bode 1873, S. 10; Bode 1883, S. 503, 602; Valentiner 1909, S. 496; Hofstede de Groot 1915, Nr 441; W. R. Valentiner, *Wiedergefundene Gemälde*, Berlin—Leipzig, 1923, S. 89, 104—105; Benesch 1935, S. 66; Левинсон-Лессинг 1956, с. XVII; Гос. Эрмитаж 1958, с. 259; Фехнер 1965, № 27; Bauch 1966, Nr 239; Gerson 1968, No 402; Bredius, No 309.

The Return of the Prodigal Son.
1636. Etching

Man Walking. Drawing.
Print Room, Amsterdam

Cornelis Antonissen. The Return
of the Prodigal Son. Engraving

28. THE RETURN OF THE PRODIGAL SON

Oil on canvas, relined. 262 × 205 cm
The original version had a rounded top; the upper corners were added later.
Near the son's feet, left, the signature (of doubtful authenticity): *Rf Rynf*.
The Hermitage, Leningrad. No 742

The evangelic parable of the prodigal son tells the story of an irresponsible youth who, taking the portion of his father's goods that fell to him, "took his journey into a far country, and there wasted his substance with riotous living". In the end, bankrupt, abandoned by false friends, after a life of suffering and disgrace, he decides to return to his father's house (*Luke*, 15. 11—32). There he finds forgiveness, love and peace.

The grand concept is embodied in a laconic and supremely expressive composition. The dominating elements are the strict vertical lines of the calm and noble figures. The father's apparel falls in broad folds, the contours of his figure embrace those of his son's,— a device emphasizing the spiritual unity of these two men and lending the group a special monumental quality.

The Return of the Prodigal Son. Lower border of the canvas
(X-ray photograph). The Hermitage, Leningrad

The figures seem to emerge from the dark background and, transfixed by light, stand amid the hot flaming colours; a lone ray, falling on the softened greens and brownish reds of the surroundings, picks out the father's bright red cloak, a symbol of passionate feelings. The lighted robes of an old man, who stands entranced by the emotions of father and son, are in harmony with the great pictorial orchestration. The complex painting, typical of Rembrandt's late period, reaches an amazing freedom and spontaneity. In the lighted areas the painting is high impasto, often applied with the spatula or finger. The surface which seems, upon close inspection, to be but a chaotic hodgepodge of dabs, becomes dazzlingly expressive at a distance. There is no generally accepted date. H. Gerson fixes it as 1661, while B. Haak holds to the traditional 1668—69. K. Bauch suggests *ca.* 1668, while H. Th. Musper believes that the painting was begun before 1650 and completed only toward the end of the 1650s. We do not think there are grounds for this point of view; the correct date is, in all probability, the early 1660s. The theme of love and charity for the suffering man, as embodied in the story of the prodigal son, was of lasting interest to Rembrandt. He returned to it time and again in his etchings and drawings.

A comparison of the Hermitage painting with the first known work by Rembrandt on this subject, his etching of 1636, inspired by the homonymous engraving of Maerten van Heemskerk, may serve as a vivid example of the artist's tremendous progress over the years. The change in concept over a thirty-year period is testified to by several drawings preserved to our days: in the Teyler Museum at Haarlem (*ca.* 1635—36), the former collection of W. R. Valentiner (*ca.* 1640), the Dresden Print Room (*ca.* 1658), the Albertina Collection in Vienna (1658—59). These drawings, however, do not provide a consistent coverage of the master's thematic interpretation, from the first etching to the Hermitage painting, although some of this painting's elements are present in the earlier works. Thus, in the Teyler Museum drawing, Rembrandt has already reorientated the son-and-father group from the profile contour of the first etching to a position where the kneeling son has his back almost completely turned to the viewer.

The composition of the painting, vertically orientated, with its elongated, static figures, differs completely from all other interpretations, just as does the lofty, nearly sanctimonious mood of the protagonists. It is especially evident in the treatment of the central group. In all previous portrayals of the father and son, the former surged forward and, as if to signify forgiveness, strove to lift his son up, while embracing and comforting him. All scenes of repentance and conciliation were depicted in a similar manner, for instance, that of Jacob and Esau, etc. Rembrandt's earlier works were no exception. In the Hermitage painting, however, the son kneels calmly, his hands clasped in prayer, while the father places his hands on his shoulders in a ges-

The Return of the Prodigal Son. Right-hand border of the canvas
(X-ray photograph). The Hermitage, Leningrad

ture of conciliation, mercy and benediction. As R. Hamann noted, the father in the painting "lays his hands on his son's shoulders as if performing a sacred rite". This new interpretation of the emotional relations between the two protagonists, which transfers these relations to a sublime and symbolic plane, appears here for the first time in Rembrandt paintings.

Rembrandt's works serve as a brilliant example of a creative interpretation of the artistic traditions of the past. The painter's main source of impressions were, in such cases, sixteenth century engravings. Sometimes (in his early period), Rembrandt would take the entire work that attracted him as a model, for instance, Maerten van Heemskerk's engraving for the etching of 1636; sometimes he chose to repeat certain compositional elements — a case in point is his *Christ before the People* (1654) and the engraving by Lucas van Leyden. At times he borrowed separate figures. There is no need to stress that in all cases this was not imitation, but a creative approach serving to give birth to works of art that, as a rule, were superior to the model. *The Return of the Prodigal Son* belongs, without doubt, to the master's late period, in the creations of which deep content is expressed through grand monumental form. Yet it would be wrong to explain the formal and moral composition of this painting, so different from all previous, by this generally applicable law. One must consider the possibility of a stimulus from without that helped Rembrandt realize his goal. This stimulus was probably an engraving on the same theme by Cornelis Antonissen.

It may be supposed that Antonissen's engraving was not new to Rembrandt; the Teyler Museum drawing, mentioned earlier, may be traced to it: differing from the Heemskerk-inspired etching of 1636, the father and son are depicted turned three quarters to the right. The composition, certain motifs and even separate details coincide in the two works; among the latter are the father's dress and the staff lying on the left. But the drawing's interpretation is in the passionate, dynamic style of Rembrandt of the 1630s. During his work on the Hermitage painting, he was much more attracted by composition and general mood.

Rembrandt turns to his early sketches for the figure of the old man on the right: his face may be seen in drawings of the mid-1630s. The old man's full-length depiction is found in the drawing *Beggar in a High Hat* (*ca.* 1636; pupil's copy?) in the Print Room of Rijksmuseum, Amsterdam. His torso, however, is turned three-quarters, not profile. The same man may be seen in the drawing *Man Walking* (in the same museum), dated *ca.* 1665 by M. Henkel, and a few years later by O. Benesch.

The canvas is horizontal-sewn and enlarged by 10—13 cm from the bottom by straightening its bent lower edge; on the right, a 10 cm wide strip of new canvas is added along the entire vertical seam. The upper corners of the painting were enlarged later (the original top was

The Return of the Prodigal Son. Head of the old man
(X-ray photograph). The Hermitage, Leningrad

rounded: see X-ray plate). Near the upper border in the middle and near the left shoulder of the standing woman there are two overpainted breaks. Small losses of the paint and priming are apparent under the father's left hand, under the son's right heel and in the right background. Numerous overpaintings can be traced along the craquelures; the lower part of the picture is repainted in black in many places.

PROVENANCE:

1742	Put up for sale with the Jan de Guis Collection in Bonn
1764	Put up for auction with the Collection of Archbishop Clemens Augustus of Bavaria; however, was not bought because of its high price
Until 1766	Duke d'Amezune Collection, Paris
1766	Acquired for the Hermitage

EXHIBITIONS:

1936	Rembrandt. Moscow—Leningrad (Cat., p. 47, No 29)
1956	Rembrandt and His School. Moscow—Leningrad (Cat., pp. 61—62)
1969—70	Rembrandt, His Precursors and Followers. Leningrad (Cat., pp. 31—32, No 24)

LITERATURE:

Hoet 1752, II, blz. 63; Имп. Эрмитаж 1863—1916, № 797; Bode 1883, S. 527—528, 600; Valentiner 1909, S. 471; Hofstede de Groot 1915, Nr 113; Weisbach 1926, S. 479—480, 513—514, 593; Benesch 1955, S. 69; К. Агафонова, «К истории композиции *Данаи* и *Блудного сына*», *Труды Государственного Эрмитажа*, I, 1940, с. 20—22; Rosenberg 1948, pp. 100, 143, 145, 197, 200, 220; Hamann 1948, S. 20, 38, 118, 196, 366, 417—418, 421, 423—424; Левинсон-Лессинг 1956, с. XIX; Knuttel 1956, blz. 44, 62, 212; Гос. Эрмитаж 1958, с. 264; Виппер 1962, с. 455, 463, 467; Levinson-Lessing 1964, No 88; Фехнер 1965, № 30; Bauch 1966, Nr 94; Gerson 1968, p. 140, No 355; H. Th. Musper, «Die Datierung von Rembrandts *Verlorenem Sohn* in Leningrad», *Festschrift für Werner Gross*, 1968, S. 229—238; Haak 1968, blz. 328—329; Bredius, No 598; W. Stechow, "The Crisis in Rembrandt Research", in: *Art Studies for an Editor: 25 Essays in Memory of Mitton S. Fox*, New York, 1975, pp. 235, 237, 238.

29. DAVID AND URIAH (?) [HAMAN ORDERED TO HONOUR MORDECAI (?)]

Oil on canvas, relined. 127 × 116 cm
Signed in the lower right-hand corner: *Rembrandt*
The Hermitage, Leningrad. No 752

In his late historical compositions Rembrandt does not strive for detailed narrative depiction. Several canvases, as the result, have been, and remain, extremely difficult to decipher. The Hermitage painting is a case in point.
From the time of its appearance in the Hermitage, the painting was called *The Downfall of Haman*. It was believed to be an illustration of the biblical episodes described in Chapters 4, 5 and 6 of the Book of Esther. The traditional interpretation of the picture was considered valid for over one and a half centuries.
In the twentieth century, however, the scholars all over the world focused their attention on this work of Rembrandt.
In 1921 W. R. Valentiner advanced the suggestion that the subject pertained to Chapter 11 (1—26) of the Second Book of Samuel. That assumption was upheld in 1956 by I. Linnik. The painting was given a new title, *David and Uriah*. The story of David and Uriah is as follows. King David seduced Bathsheba, the wife of the soldier Uriah. Trying to get rid of the deceived husband, David sent Uriah to the war and gave him a letter for his commander Joab. The letter contained a message demanding that Uriah be sent to the forefront of the battle. Uriah feels that death is imminent but, not wishing to lose his honour, he silently leaves the King.
This interpretation of the Hermitage painting finds corroboration in both the psychological atmosphere and the choice of personages depicted (the old man at the left is the scribe who wrote the King's message). However, this version, too, has its weak points: first, the letter itself is absent (although one might suppose it is hidden in the folds of Uriah's garments or that he is pressing it in his hand); second, the splendid dress of the main character betrays his high title, something which does not fit Uriah.
In 1957 W. R. Valentiner advanced yet another interpretation: *Jonathan Leaving Saul's Banquet* (*1 Samuel*, 20. 24—34). However, the state of mind of the picture's protagonists — the King's calm sorrow and Jonathan's horror — is not enough to warrant this interpretation.
In 1911 Hofstede de Groot interpreted the traditional title, *The Downfall of Haman*, as pertaining to Chapter 6, not Chapter 7, of the Book of Esther (see his *Rembrandt's Bible*). In 1961—65 F. Abel and M. Kahr came to the same conclusion, which found Ch. Tümpel's support in 1968.
The subject in view is as follows.
Mordecai, Queen Esther's uncle and teacher, uncovered a plot against King Ahasuerus. For this Mordecai's name was entered in the "book of records of the chronicles", but he was given no reward. Mordecai was a proud and independent man. He was the only one who refused to bow down to the all-powerful minister Haman, and the latter hated him for this. One night the King could not sleep, and he ordered that the "book of records of the chronicles" be brought to him. When the story of Mordecai's deed was read to him, the King asked what honour or dignity had been bestowed on him. Learning that no such thing had been done, the King called his minister and asked, "What shall be done unto the man whom the king delighteth to honour?" Haman, thinking the King had him in mind, replied that such a man should be clothed in royal apparel, taken on horseback through the streets and acclaimed. The King agreed and ordered him to do thus unto Mordecai. Haman left the King in a state of anger, consternation and with a sense of ill-boding. This story is also told by Josephus Fla-

vius in his *Hebrew Antiquities*, a book which was in Rembrandt's possession (this is documentally proved) and in which Haman's state of mourning is underlined even more strongly than in the Bible. In what concerns the third protagonist, the old man to the left, Ch. Tümpel suggests that this is Mordecai. But nowhere does the biblical text mention Mordecai being brought before the King; neither does Josephus Flavius mention this. The Bible, to the contrary, specifies that Ahasuerus ordered Haman to honour "Mordecai the Jew, that sitteth at the king's gate"; it was back to this very gate that Mordecai returned after his triumph, he did not enter the palace. Mordecai had the honour to appear before the King only after Haman's death, and even then only when Ahasuerus learned that Mordecai was Esther's uncle (*Esther*, 8. 1).

A wealth of examples show Rembrandt to have been well versed in the iconographic traditions of the sixteenth century. Therefore Ch. Tümpel has every reason, when considering the third personage in the painting, to refer to Philipp Halle's engraving *Ahasuerus Orders Haman to Honour Mordecai* after Maerten van Heemskerk. However, he probably errs in this case. The left foreground of this engraving depicts the moment when the "book of records" is being read and Ahasuerus speaks to Haman, while on the right we see the subsequent triumph of Mordecai. In the left background we see two men engaged in earnest discussion. Ch. Tümpel interprets them as servants inviting Mordecai to the palace. This, however, contradicts the Bible, and the conduct of these two gives no reason for such an interpretation. Even if, for argument's sake, we agree that the third personage of Rembrandt's picture is Mordecai, then where is Haman going? The King could not have sent him to fetch Mordecai, for Mordecai is already there. From the point of view of psychology there is even less reason to interpret the sorrowful old man as Mordecai. The King's order could hardly have been a cause for sorrow — Haman was the sworn enemy of Mordecai and his people. For Mordecai such honour, accorded to him by the King, could only be a reason for joy, for it gave hope of saving his people from their tragic fate — Mordecai's most fervent wish.

The riddle of the third personage has yet to find an answer, for it is hard to understand who could be so grief-stricken by the King's order (the old man in the picture is nearly crying). No one could have possibly interpreted the King's order as the beginning of Haman's downfall: even after Esther unmasked Haman's plot, Ahasuerus hesitated to condemn his favourite minister; he took the decision only when he suspected Haman of attempting to force the Queen. Only Haman himself, with his guilty conscience and wounded pride, could have received the order with foreboding. So Ch. Tümpel has no grounds to speak of the "horror and pity" of the personages in the background — at that moment there was no room for such emotions. What could have been the reason for sorrow on the King's part? That his favourite minister had gone to obey an order which would give him, the King, only a sense of satisfaction with a duty fulfilled?

M. Kahr explains the King's sad expression as remorse at having forgotten about Mordecai's deed and thus having been unjust. Such high moral standards are hardly plausible in an Oriental potentate who enjoys his meat and wine after having ordered the extermination of an entire people, "all Jews, both young and old, little children and women" (*Esther*, 3. 12—15); but even so, such emotions might have manifested themselves before his order to honour Mordecai, not after, when he repaid the old Jew in what he considered royal fashion.

The red cloth on Haman's left shoulder speaks in favour of the last interpretation: it can be taken for the royal garment Ahasuerus ordered to be given to Mordecai. Such a supposition is all the more plausible because Josephus Flavius makes special mention of the King's purple apparel. Yet Haman does not carry in his hands the King's gold chain, twice mentioned by Josephus Flavius. Without doubt, Rembrandt, who in that period paid little attention to accessories, might have omitted that detail. But we see that very same chain hanging from the King's neck, although royalty would have been evident enough in the crowned turban and ermine-lined golden cape.

In 1967 I. Nieuwstraten argued against the interpretation of the Hermitage painting as *Haman Ordered to Honour Mordecai*. Not agreeing with earlier versions, he suggests that the painting, as we see it today, differs seriously from the original: parts were cut off and lost, and without these missing fragments it is impossible, according to him, to solve the mystery.

Study of the canvas lining along the edges, however, does not confirm this hypothesis. It would be wrong, therefore, to speak of personages or details which have disappeared and which could have helped the solution.

A slight distortion of the canvas, when transferred to a new subframe, has made all the figures incline somewhat to the right. Originally, the personages in the background were more vertical, while the central figure was bent even more to the left, thus stressing the unsteady character of its movement. This figure is one of Rembrandt's most expressive both as a psychological study and with regard to the beauty and perfection of the brushwork. The livid lips, the sunken, greyish face clouded, as it were, by death, seem crushed by the huge dazzling turban. The face seems particularly small and helpless in contrast to the resplendent purple apparel, where the combination of variegated reds and ochres creates a strikingly intense colouring.

The portrayal of the two other personages differs in manner. The colour scheme is changed and the psychological key is somewhat simplified. It would seem as though the artist put his entire soul into the main protagonist, while the rest interested him as a kind of accompaniment to the latter's emotions. A comparison of the scale of the figures adds to this feeling of incongruity. The background figures are smaller than the perspective calls for.

Evidently this incompatibility led some scholars to question Rembrandt's authorship where the background figures are concerned. The differing "handwriting" of the brushwork in the foreground and background figures certainly leaves room for such doubts.

The majority of scholars date the painting about 1665.

The painting's condition is good. There are two large breaks in the paint in the left lower corner.

PROVENANCE:

1734   Probably sold on May 13 at an auction of the V. Six Collection in Amsterdam
Until 1769   Blackwood Collection, London
1769   Acquired for the Hermitage

EXHIBITIONS:

1936   Rembrandt. Moscow—Leningrad (Cat., p. 47, No 27)
1956   Rembrandt and His School. Moscow—Leningrad (Cat., p. 61)
1969—70   Rembrandt, His Precursors and Followers. Leningrad (Cat., pp. 30—31, No 23)
1975—76   Master Paintings from the Hermitage and the State Russian Museum, Leningrad. Washington, D.C.; New York, N.Y.; Detroit, Michigan; Los Angeles, California; Houston, Texas (Cat. No 19)
1976   Master Paintings from the Hermitage and the Russian Museum, Leningrad. Mexico (Cat. No 19)
1976   Master Paintings from the Hermitage and State Russian Museum, Leningrad. Winnipeg (Cat. No 19)

LITERATURE:

Имп. Эрмитаж 1863—1916, № 795; Bode 1883, S. 479; Valentiner 1909, S. 469; Hofstede de Groot, 1915, Nr 48; Weisbach 1926, S. 476, 594; Hamann 1948, S. 412—413; Левинсон-Лессинг 1956, с. XIX; Knuttel 1956, blz. 208; И. Линник, «К вопросу о сюжете картины Рембрандта в собрании Эрмитажа», *Искусство*, 1956, № 7, с. 46—50; J. Białostocki, «Ikonographische Forschungen zu Rembrandts Werk», *Münchner Jahrbuch der bildenden Kunst*, VIII, 1957, S. 210; И. Линник, «О сюжете картины Рембрандта, известной под названием *Падение Амана*», *Сообщения Государственного Эрмитажа*, XI, 1957, с. 8—12; Гос. Эрмитаж 1958, с. 259; А. Членов, «К вопросу о сюжете картины Рембрандта *Давид и Урия*», *Искусство*, 1958, № 10, с. 60—62; Виппер 1962, с. 454—456; Levinson-Lessing 1964, No 84; M. Kahr, "A Rembrandt Problem: Haman or Uriah?", *Journal of the Warburg and Courtauld Institute*, 28, 1965, pp. 258—273; Фехнер 1965, № 29; Bauch 1966, Nr 39; I. Nieuwstraten, "Haman, Rembrandt and Michelangelo", *Oud-Holland*, LXXXII, 1967, blz. 61—63; M. Kahr, "Rembrandt's Meaning", *Oud-Holland*, LXXXIII, 1968, blz. 63—68; Ch. Tümpel, «Ikonographische Beiträge zu Rembrandt», *Jahrbuch der Hamburger Kunstsammlungen*, 13, 1968, S. 106—112; Gerson 1968, No 357; Bredius, No 531; J. Held, *Rembrandt's* Aristotle *and Other Rembrandt Studies*, Princeton, 1969, p. 30; E. Panofsky, "Comments on Art and Reformation", in: *Symbols in Transformation* (exhibition catalogue), The Art Museum, Princeton University, 1969, p. 14; H. van de Waal, "Rembrandt and the Feast of Purim", *Oud-Holland*, 1969, blz. 199—223; A. Bader, "A New Interpretation of Rembrandt's *Disgrace of Haman*", *The Burlington Magazine*, August 1971, pp. 473—474; J. Białostocki, «Der Sünder als tragischer Held bei Rembrandt», in: *Neue Beiträge zur Rembrandt-Forschung* (hrsg. von O. von Simson und J. Kelch), Berlin, 1973, S. 138—140; J. Białostocki, *Rembrandt's Iconography: Rembrandt after Three Hundred Years* (Symposium, October 22—24, 1969), Art Institute of Chicago, 1973, p. 75; J. Held, D. Posner, *Seventeenth and Eighteenth Century Art*, New York, 1973, p. 266; Yu. Kuznetsov, "Rembrandt Discoveries at the Hermitage", *Apollo*, December 1974, pp. 486—488; W. Stechow, "The Crisis in Rembrandt Research", in: *Art Studies for an Editor: 25 Essays in Memory of Mitton S. Fox*, New York, 1975, pp. 235—239.

30. PORTRAIT OF THE POET JEREMIAS DE DECKER

Oil on oak, cradled. 71 × 56 cm
Signed and dated at bottom, right: *Rembrandt f. 1666*
The Hermitage, Leningrad. No 748

Jeremias de Decker was one of Holland's most gifted poets of the seventeenth century. Of the same age as Rembrandt, he was born in Dordrecht in 1606, moved to Amsterdam while still young, and died there in 1666. His childhood was hard: he lost many of his relatives at an early age. As one Dutch scholar wrote, "he had little reason to smile — and so he smiled not. The dominating feature of his nature is gravity. His gentleness at times changes to sorrow, even to gloom, a gloom engendering in him a wish to die... But this never makes him bitter or misanthropic. No, his sorrow and gravity are tempered with kindness originating in his deep faith, his humanism, the attractive gentleness of his emotions, qualities so rarely found among other Dutch poets of the seventeenth century." These words can serve as a kind of clue to Rembrandt's portrait representing an elderly, thoughtful man with sad and tired eyes.

From his very youth, Rembrandt was a close friend of Decker. In his poem dedicated to Rembrandt's *Christ the Gardener* (Buckingham Palace, London), Decker described his impressions of Rembrandt at work on this picture, finished in 1668: "My friend Rembrandt, I was the first to see your masterly strokes running down that panel." Interesting to note, Decker goes beyond the traditional praise and description of the painting, and speaks of the cliff "rich in shadings" that lends a solemn atmosphere to the entire scene: the poet was probably one of the few who gave Rembrandt's chiaroscuro its due. Rembrandt painted *Christ the Gardener* for Decker's friend, the poet H. Waterloos. Waterloos's poem, published in 1660 on the occasion of Rembrandt completing a portrait of Jeremias de Decker, testifies to the existence of yet another portrait of this man, done by Rembrandt at an earlier stage.

The *Portrait of Jeremias de Decker* of the Hermitage collection is rather unusual. The poet's face is enveloped in deep shadow through which the features are more guessed at than seen: the hooded eyes look strangely back at us as if from a great depth. Remembering that the painting is dated the year of the poet's death, we cannot help wondering if this is not a requiem for a gone or going friend. Strictly speaking, the portrait is unfinished: only the head and upper part of the chest are painted in detail, the body and arm being only roughly sketched. The painting is in good condition. To the right of the face, on the background, overpainting was applied over an early loss of paint.

PROVENANCE:

1696	Probably mentioned in the inventory of Jeronimus Swerts' widow
Until 1782	Baudouin Collection, Paris
1782	Acquired for the Hermitage

EXHIBITIONS:

1936	Rembrandt. Moscow—Leningrad (Cat., p. 47, No 28)
1956	Rembrandt. Amsterdam—Rotterdam (Cat. No 97)
1969—70	Rembrandt, His Precursors and Followers. Leningrad (Cat., p. 30, No 22)

LITERATURE:

Имп. Эрмитаж 1863—1916, № 827; Bode 1883, S. 538, 603; N. de Roever, «Rembrandt», *Oud-Holland*, II, 1884, blz. 85, 86; Valentiner 1909, S. 508; K. H. de Raaf, «Rembrandt's portret van Jeremias Decker», *Oud-Holland*, XXX, 1912, blz. 1—5; A. Bredius, «Bij Rembrandt's portret van Jeremias de Decker», *Oud-Holland*, XXXI, 1913, blz. 272; Hofstede de Groot 1915, Nr 776; Weisbach 1926, S. 42; A. Bredius, *The Paintings of Rembrandt*, Vienna, 1935, p. 69; S. Slive, *Rembrandt and His Critics: 1630—1730*, The Hague, 1953, pp. 46—49; Левинсон-Лессинг 1956, с. XVII; Knuttel 1956, blz. 220; Гос. Эрмитаж 1958, с. 264; Виппер 1962, с. 455; Levinson-Lessing 1964, No 87; Фехнер 1965, № 28; Bauch 1966, Nr 442; Gerson 1968, No 413; Haak 1969, blz. 323; Bredius, No 320.

ABBREVIATIONS

Aedes Walpolianae	*Aedes Walpolianae, or a Description of the Collection of Pictures at Houghton Hall in Norfolk, the Seat of the Right Honourable Robert Walpole, Earl of Orford*, 2nd ed., London, 1752
Bartsch	A. Bartsch, *Catalogue raisonné de toutes les estampes qui forment l'œuvre de Rembrandt et ceux de ses principaux imitateurs*, vol. I—II, Vienne, 1797
Bauch 1933	K. Bauch, *Die Kunst des jungen Rembrandt*, Heidelberg, 1933
Bauch 1960	K. Bauch, *Der frühe Rembrandt und seine Zeit*, Berlin, 1960
Bauch 1966	K. Bauch, *Rembrandt. Gemälde*, Berlin, 1966
Benesch	O. Benesch, *The Drawings of Rembrandt*, vol. I—VII, London, 1954—57
Benesch 1935	O. Benesch, *Rembrandt. Werk und Forschung*, Wien, 1935
Bode 1873	W. Bode, *Die Gemäldegalerie in der Kaiserlichen Eremitage. Meisterwerke der holländischen Schule*, St Petersburg, 1873
Bode 1883	W. Bode, *Studien zur Geschichte der holländischen Malerei*, Braunschweig, 1883
Bode—Hofstede de Groot 1897—1905	W. Bode, C. Hofstede de Groot, *Rembrandt. Beschreibendes Verzeichnis seiner Gemälde*, Paris, 1897—1905
Bredius	A. Bredius, *Rembrandt. The Complete Edition of the Paintings* (revised by H. Gerson), London, 1969 (1st ed. 1935)
Catalogue 1774	E. Munich, *Catalogue raisonné des tableaux qui se trouvent dans les Galeries et Cabinets du Palais Impérial à Saint-Pétersbourg*, Saint-Pétersbourg, 1774
Gerson 1968	H. Gerson, *Rembrandt Paintings*, Amsterdam, 1968
Haak 1968	B. Haak, *Rembrandt. Zijn leven, zijn werk, zijn tijd*, Amsterdam, 1968
Hamann 1948	R. Hamann, *Rembrandt*, Potsdam, 1948
Hoet 1752	G. Hoet, *Catalogus of Naamlijst van schilderijen, met derselven prijzen...*, D. I—II, 's-Gravenhage, 1752
Hofstede de Groot	C. Hofstede de Groot, *Die Handzeichnungen Rembrandts. Versuch eines beschreibenden und kritischen Katalogs*, Haarlem, 1906
Hofstede de Groot 1915	C. Hofstede de Groot, *Beschreibendes und kritisches Verzeichnis der Werke hervorragendsten holländischen Maler des XVII. Jahrhunderts*, Bd. VI, Esslingen—Paris, 1915

Knuttel 1956	G. Knuttel, *Rembrandt. De meester en zijn werk*, Amsterdam, 1956
Levinson-Lessing 1964	V. F. Levinson-Lessing, *The Hermitage, Leningrad: Dutch and Flemish Masters*, London, 1964
Livret 1838	*Livret de la Galerie Impériale de l'Ermitage de Saint-Pétersbourg*, Saint-Pétersbourg, 1838
Notice 1828	*Notice sur les principaux tableaux au Musée Impérial de l'Ermitage à Saint-Pétersbourg*, Saint-Pétersbourg, 1828
Rosenberg 1948	J. Rosenberg, *Rembrandt*, vol. I—II, Cambridge (Mass.), 1948
Terwesten 1770	P. Terwesten, *Catalogus of Naamlijst van schilderijen, met derzelven prijzen...*, 's-Gravenhage, 1770
Valentiner 1909	W. R. Valentiner, *Rembrandt. Des Meisters Gemälde*, 3. Aufl., Stuttgart—Leipzig, 1909
Waagen 1864	G. Waagen, *Die Gemäldesammlung in der Kaiserlichen Eremitage zu St Petersburg...*, München, 1864
Weisbach 1926	W. Weisbach, *Rembrandt*, Berlin, 1926
Альбом ГМИИ 1966	*Государственный музей изобразительных искусств им. А. С. Пушкина. Западноевропейская живопись и скульптура (альбом)*, Москва, 1966
Виппер 1957	Б. Р. Виппер, *Становление реализма в голландской живописи XVII века*, Москва, 1957
Виппер 1962	Б. Р. Виппер, *Очерки голландской живописи эпохи расцвета*, Москва, 1962
Вольская 1966	В. Н. Вольская, «Рембрандт и барокко», в сб.: *Классическое искусство за рубежом*, Москва, 1966
Гос. Эрмитаж 1958	*Государственный Эрмитаж. Отдел западноевропейского искусства. Каталог живописи*, т. 2, Москва—Ленинград, 1958
Егорова 1966	К. С. Егорова, «Портреты в творчестве Рембрандта 1650-х годов», в сб.: *Классическое искусство за рубежом*, Москва, 1966
Имп. Эрмитаж 1863—1916	*Императорский Эрмитаж. Каталог картин*, Петербург—Петроград, 1863—1916
Исследование картин Рембрандта	М. П. Виктурина, А. Л. Дуб, К. С. Егорова, «Исследование картин Рембрандта», в сб.: *Памятники культуры. Новые открытия. Письменность, искусство, археология*, Москва, 1975
Каталог ГМИИ 1961	*Государственный музей изобразительных искусств им. А. С. Пушкина. Каталог картинной галереи*, Москва, 1961
Лазарев 1936	В. Н. Лазарев, «Проблема портрета у Рембрандта», *Искусство*, 1936, № 6
Левинсон-Лессинг 1956	В. Ф. Левинсон-Лессинг, *Рембрандт ван Рейн*, Москва, 1956
Ротенберг 1956	Е. Ротенберг, *Рембрандт Гарменс ван Рейн*, Москва, 1956
Сомов 1893	А. Сомов, *Императорский Эрмитаж. Каталог картинной галереи*, т. 2 (Нидерландская и немецкая живопись), Петербург, 1893 (2-е изд. 1902)
Фехнер 1965	Е. Ю. Фехнер, *Рембрандт. Произведения живописи в музеях СССР*, Ленинград—Москва, 1965

BIOGRAPHICAL OUTLINE

1606	Rembrandt Harmensz van Rijn born on 15th July, in Leyden, the son of Harmen Gerritsz van Rijn, miller
ca. 1613—20	Studies at the Latin school in Leyden
1620	20th May: Rembrandt's name appears on the roll of Leyden University
ca. 1621—24	Period of apprenticeship: three years with Jacob Isaaksz van Swanenburgh in Leyden
ca. 1624—25	Six months with Pieter Lastman in Amsterdam
ca. 1625	Establishes his own workshop in Leyden
1625—31	Works together with his friend Jan Lievens
1626	*Christ Driving the Money-changers from the Temple*
1628	Gerard Dou becomes Rembrandt's pupil
1630	Death of Rembrandt's father, buried in Leyden on 27th April
1631	Rembrandt settles in Amsterdam, in the house of the art dealer Hendrick van Uylenburgh *Portrait of a Scholar*
1632	*The Anatomy Lesson of Doctor Tulp*
1633—39	Works on a series of paintings of the *Passions* for the Stadholder, Prince Frederick Henry of Orange
1634	Marriage to Saskia van Uylenburgh, on 10th July *Saskia as Flora*
Until 1635	Jacob Backer, Govaert Flinck and Ferdinand Bol study at Rembrandt's workshop
1635	*Abraham's Sacrifice*
ca. 1636	Buys an apartment in Nieuwe Dollenstraat
1636	First version of *Danaë*
1637	*The Parable of the Labourers in the Vineyard*
1639	Rembrandt buys a house in Jodenbreestraat where he collects a large number of paintings, prints and etchings
Until 1640	Gerbrandt van den Eeckhout studies at Rembrandt's workshop
1640	Death of Rembrandt's mother, buried in Leyden on 14th September
1641	22nd September: baptism of Rembrandt's son Titus

1642	14th June: death of Saskia, buried in the Oud Kerk, Amsterdam, on 18th June *The Night Watch* *David's Farewell to Jonathan*
1643—49	Geertge Dircx documented in Rembrandt's household
Until 1645	Carel Fabritius, Lambert Doomer, Samuel van Hoogstraaten, and Jurian Ovens study at Rembrandt's workshop
1645	*The Holy Family with Angels*
ca. 1646—47	Second version of *Danaë*
1649—63	Hendrickje Stoffels documented in Rembrandt's household
Until 1650	Nicolas Maes, Bernard Fabritius and Willem Drost study at Rembrandt's workshop
1652	Rembrandt receives a commission from Antonio Ruffo, a patron of art from Sicily, to paint *Aristotle Contemplating a Bust of Homer* (finished in 1653)
1654	30th October: baptism of Hendrickje's daughter, Cornelia
1656	Inventory of Rembrandt's possessions made on the occasion of his bankruptcy *The Anatomy Lesson of Doctor Joan Deijman*
1657	Sale of Rembrandt's collections *Young Woman with Earrings*
1658	Sale of Rembrandt's house. The family moves to Rosengracht where Hendrickje and Titus carry on an independent art-dealing business
1659	*Christ and the Woman of Samaria*
ca. 1660	Aert de Gelder, the last pupil of Rembrandt, studies at his workshop
1660	*Ahasuerus, Haman and Esther*
1661	Antonio Ruffo buys Rembrandt's *Alexander the Great* and commissions a portrait of Homer
1661—62	*The Conspiracy of Claudius Civilis: The Oath*
1662	*The Board of the Drapers' Guild*
ca. 1663	*The Return of the Prodigal Son*
1663	Death of Hendrickje Stoffels, buried in the Westerkerk, Amsterdam, on 24th July
ca. 1665	*David and Uriah* (?)
1666	*Portrait of the Poet Jeremias de Decker*
1668	Death of Titus, who had married Magdalena van Loo on 10th February; buried in the Westerkerk, Amsterdam, on 7th September
1669	22nd March: baptism of Rembrandt's granddaughter Titia. Rembrandt works on *Simeon in the Temple*, his last unfinished painting 4th October: death of Rembrandt 8th October: buried in the Westerkerk, Amsterdam

LIST OF ILLUSTRATIONS

PLATES

ILLUSTRATIONS IN THE CATALOGUE

РЕМБРАНДТ
Альбом (на английском языке)
Издательство «Аврора». Ленинград. 1981
По заказу фирмы
Harry N. Abrams, Inc., Publishers, New York
Изд. № 3320. Printed and bound in the USSR